THE SPLENDID ART

The
Splendid Art
A HISTORY OF THE OPERA

Thomas Matthews

CROWELL-COLLIER PRESS
Collier-Macmillan Limited, London

Library of Congress Catalog Card Number: 78-93717

The Macmillan Company
866 Third Avenue
New York, New York 10022

Collier-Macmillan Canada Ltd., Toronto, Ontario

Printed in the United States of America

First Printing

For
CAROLINA SEGRERA,
a prima donna of elegance and wisdom
who gives so much to the young artists of today.

She is the inspiration that composers,
singers, and writers dream of

Contents

THE SPLENDID ART

CHAPTER ONE

Some Questions and Answers About Opera

What is opera? Where did it begin? Is it a dusty institution that was born in ancient Greece, was nurtured in Renaissance Italy, and is doomed to die in our times? Does a musical form that gained its foothold in the gilded splendor of 1597 Venice, and captured all of the civilized world, find itself compatible with the glowing, psychedelic atmosphere of modern San Francisco, London, Paris, and New York? *Who* and what strange fascinations have kept opera alive? Is it—like the theater, the movies, television, and all entertainment—a necessary escape?

The last question has been answered convincingly by the gifted English writer Jonathan Griffin. He believes that if opera, or any work of art, provides an escape, it is fulfilling a need. "For *young people* who will grow up, to them, in or approaching the world of policy and action, it offers a reminder, too strong to be forgotten, that there is more to man's or woman's life than conforming for the sake of earning money and status; a reinforcement or restoration of one's power to be uncorrupted by one's conforming—not to conform all the way.

Political reality makes some shattering appearances in the opera house. What work of any kind or period causes a more searing feeling of the difference between being free and being oppressed, than *Fidelio?* Of the nature of social tyranny than *Figaro?* Of hopeless poverty than *Wozzeck?"*

Grove's Dictionary of Music and Musicians defines opera as "a drama, either tragic or comic, sung throughout, to the accompaniment of an orchestra, with appropriate scenery and acting." Accordingly, a history of opera, in addition to being informative about its composers, should attempt to throw some light on *all* the vital ingredients that, when successfully combined, make opera an exciting theatrical entertainment.

A history of opera should also explain some of the mystery, the glamour, the adulation attached to singers. And what is the lure of opera that has motivated Maria Callas, the most influential prima donna of our time, to say, *"Singing* for me is not an act of pride, but merely an attempt to rise towards those heights where everything is harmony."

An analysis of opera must consider the singer as an actor, the orchestra, costumes, and scenery.

Drama is as old as Greece, and opera is a product of drama. Sophocles and Aeschylus might be considered the first opera librettists because their plays were accompanied by flutes and lyres. The great plays of that time had not only leading and supporting actors but choruses. These choruses entoned their speeches and narratives. The actual pitch and tone of the actors' voices were raised and lowered for dramatic effect.

Scholars over the years have ascertained that Greek singing was never harmonic. The actors sang and the orchestra played the identical melody.

Music was of major importance in the lives of the Greeks. In fact, all of Greek education was encased in one word—*mousike* (music).

Antigone was one of the popular successes in ancient Greece, as was *Electra,* whose story is the basis of one of Richard Strauss's enduring operatic triumphs, *Elektra.* These dramas have lived through the centuries in many forms. *Antigonae* may be heard today as a *World-Theater* work by Carl Orff. His setting, however, is attuned to twentieth-century ears—it utilizes an ochestra of percussion instruments and six pianos.

There were those, of course, who believed that the beginning of opera—the musical entoning of a drama—was a violation of established theatrical tradition. As with all peoples and with all histories, to be *new* was tampering and falsifying. Truth be known, the "singing" of passages brought a color and depth of feeling to these Greek plays that the speaking voice had failed to do.

However, this early beginning was just a beginning. It was not until 1597 that the first *opera in musica* (work in music) was presented.

As the sixteenth century came to a close, the Greek style of musical declamation continued to intrigue Italian musicians. Friends of Count Giovanni Bardi, in particular, were determined to revitalize this ancient form and add another dimension to it. These inquiring and artistic men were dominated by the urge to create something new and adventurous in music. The Camerata—as they named their group—was comprised of musicians, poets, a singer, a shopkeeper, and a lute player whose other claim to fame was that he was the father of Galileo Galilei, the astronomer.

Two of the Camerata's younger members, Jacopo Peri and Giulio Caccini, were blessed with exceptionally inventive minds and were determined to do away with anything that smacked of tradition. They were convinced that there had to be a way of composing music that would allow them to express themselves *and* the basic human emotions of the people of their time. Count Bardi, the inspirational leader of the Camerata, made certain that encouragement and assistance were always at hand.

The inquisitive ambitions of the Camerata led its members to the invention of a work for one singer accompanied by one instrument. This limited but new form of composition was called a cantata.

Peri's search proceeded along still more inventive lines, and in 1597 his *opera* (*Dramma per la musica*), *Dafne,* was produced at the Palazzo Corsi. Its striking success led to a royal commission. He was asked to create a musical presentation to follow the wedding of Henry IV of France and Maria de' Medici. For his drama Peri chose a poem, *Orpheus and Eurydice,* by one of his Camerata colleagues, Ottavio Rinuccini. Its poetry supplied the composer with the vital themes that interested him most—love and death. A nobleman by the name of Corsi was at the harpsichord for this first performance of *Euridice*. It is certain that neither he nor the other musicians (three flutes, two lutes, and a bass viol) participating in the melodious birth of a musical form could have suspected that centuries later some of these same instruments would be used as "new " instrumentation for the formidable rock groups of the twentieth century.

With the successful *Euridice* the two Camerata collaborators had advanced the idea of drama with music into a theatrical work that more or less resembles what is known as opera today.

Despite their cleverness and their success, Peri and Caccini were no competition for the genius of Claudio Monteverdi (1567–1643). By the time he was twenty, Monteverdi had written a book of madrigals (a type of contrapuntal composition for several voices) in which emotion and atmosphere are conveyed—by way of bold, unflinching chords and rhythms—with amazing crispness and fidelity. Monteverdi had a feeling for theater, and he thought nothing of breaking rules. With his opera *Orfeo* (Mantua, 1607), the composer did more than break rules. He scored his work for a larger orchestra than any of his predecessors had dreamed of using. His daring use of thirty, sometimes forty musicians was an innovation that would ultimately encourage future composers to score their works for more than one hundred instruments. Although many agree that *Orfeo* is not a complete original, Monteverdi's ability and determination to stress the personal feelings of people in his music are indisputable contributions to all opera. His last work for the theater, *L'incoronazione di Poppea* (*The Coronation of Poppea*), written when he was seventy-five, is without a doubt the foundation of the opera style that was soon to fascinate and engulf all of Italy.

In addition, his successful experiments with instruments revitalized the whole idea of the potential of the orchestra. He was the first composer to consider seriously the necessity of a *balance* between instruments. Before him, composers cared little if the fragile lutes were overwhelmed by the heavy bass viols. They were even less concerned with the incongruity of allowing trumpets to characterize the frenzied demons of Hades *and* a poor, lost wood nymph. It was Monteverdi who devised the idea of having the brass and the winds be the musical conjurers of strong emotions and scenes of war. He relegated tenderness and romantic love to the softer strings.

In its early, formative years, opera was the exclusive property and delight of the nobility. Wealthy patronage was an absolute necessity if the costs of mounting the increasingly extravagant productions were to be met. Opera was the fashionable thing for sixteenth- and seventeenth-century rulers. They derived great pleasure from the rivalry of outdoing one another and allowing their favorite composers complete freedom. The more spectacular the settings and the ballets, the better. Due to this wealthy patronage, it took more than forty years for opera to become a part of public entertainment. Opera, with the help of Monteverdi, flourished in Venice and Mantua. Then it moved on to conquer Rome.

The first notable success in that city was still another version of the Orpheus legend—Stefano Landi's (c. 1581–c. 1650) *La Morte d'Orfeo* (*The Death of Orpheus*). It was a sumptuous work and overflowing with innumerable displays of vocal virtuosity. But the composer had definitely not patterned his work after Monteverdi's. Landi created music that did nothing to convey human passions or interpret human motives.

In 1626, Domenico Mazzocchi's *La catene d'Adore* (*The Chain of Adonis*) was performed for the first time in Rome, and its score discloses the term *aria*. It is an Italian word meaning *air* or *song*. The different types of arias will be discussed in another chapter on singing and musical terms. It is mentioned now only as being historically significant and stemming from this Roman period.

As exclusive as these nobility-supported court operas may have been intended, an Italian, Pietro della Valle, wrote in 1640 that a new lyric form was making some headway with the masses. He describes a group of masked performers as they enacted a play which had been set to music. During carnival time they traveled from street to street with a little cart and stage. Their performances appear to have been an unqualified success, for they played to what we call "Standing Room Only" audiences from four in the afternoon until the clocks were striking twelve. There is little doubt that these traveling singers could not begin to duplicate the glamorous style of the productions sponsored by the nobility, but they were impressing a music-hungry public. Indeed, their rustic, portable stage didn't pretend to compare with the ornate Barberini Theater in Rome which had a seating capacity of three thousand. This theater, a part of the Barberini Palace, whose occupants were princes of the powerful Church of Rome, was the scene of many an important operatic premiere.

The first public theater is said to have been built in Venice. It was called the San Cassiano and opera singers trod the boards there several years before Monteverdi died. Imagine if you will, though, these dramas of love and death being performed in a setting that in no way resembled the palaces and homes of the nobility. The San Cassiano was a theater equipped with the barest essentials. It completely lacked ventilation; there were benches instead of chairs, and the place was rarely cleaned. The devoted operagoer of those early days must have been strong of heart and nose. Things improved.

The Church of Rome displayed little approval of the turn opera was taking, and made it quite plain that secular themes were frowned upon. This dogmatic preference for religious ideas and the oratorio form did much to delay the projection of any kind of comedy into the opera theater. Oratorio originated around 1600 in the Oratory of St. Philip Neri. It is a musical composition with religious text, written for orchestra, soloists, and chorus. It requires no scenery or dramatic action.

Since comedy and laughter are as much a part of everyday living as tragedy and tears, it was to be expected that comic opera would eventually come to life. It did—during the seventeenth century.

Inasmuch as the Holy City has been taken to task for delaying comedy in opera, it must now be given some credit. The Camerata innovated the cantata and the recitative, a kind of speech-song, developed the solo aria, and Rome awakened composers to the power of the chorus. Choruses, due, in no little way, to the abundance of wonderful choirs and church schools in that city, eventually became the feature attraction of Roman operatic music. The chorus is today an important part of the majority of operas.

The popular appeal of opera was first seen in Venice. This new entertainment entranced the people of the city to such an extent that just a little more than fifty years passed before seventeen opera houses in Venice had produced more than four hundred operas. Opera houses sprang up with each decade until—between 1650 and 1700—Venice's population of 125,000 was able to afford six opera companies the luxury of operating simultaneously for seasons that extended into thirty weeks each year.

Opera's popularity increased, and other changes took place. The use of the chorus, so brilliantly established by the Romans, slowly began to disappear. The populace that came to be entertained cared less and less for cumbersome masses of chorus singers and the managers found themselves face to face with a dilemma that continues to exist today. Incredible amounts of money were needed for the upkeep of great choral groups. Also, the public's appetite had been whetted for a type of "star" that remains unequaled today—the virtuoso singer.

Opera was affected now, for the first time (and not the last), by the demands of box-office appeal. If opera was to pay, impresarios had to be considerate of those who bought tickets. The condescension of the nobility and the intelligent aristocracy had to make way for, or at least pay attention to, the demands of the people. The new public was demanding more melody, more songs, invigorating rhythms, and a clearness of expression that had not been made evident.

These changes and the new-felt power of the people did not, however, cause the baroque court opera to disappear overnight. A typical readjustment period produced one of the ideal examples of opera in the grand style—Marc' Antonio Cesti's *Il Pomo d'Oro* (*The Golden Apple*). It was composed in 1667 for the spectacular wedding that joined Leopold I of Austria and the Infanta Margarita of Spain. The royal court of Austria, with no intention of taking second place to Louis XIV's golden Versailles, staged Cesti's opera in sixty-five scenes. Twenty-four elegant sets were used—many that required extremely complicated stage machinery.

Cesti's extravaganza was only one of the never-ending celebrations and festive events that lasted for more than six months —all paying honor to the Emperor and his new bride. A special theater had to be built to house the grandiose cast of sing-

ers and actors which numbered one thousand. This little whim
of noble minds cost the fantastic amount of 100,000 gulden.

One of the most important musicians and contributors to
opera during this century was Alessandro Scarlatti (1659–1725).
His first opera was produced in Rome in 1679, and its success
brought him to the attention of Queen Christina of Sweden
who was living in the Holy City at the time. She was so
impressed with Scarlatti that she openly defied representatives
of the Pope and offered the composer her royal protection.
The story is that Scarlatti was in poor favor with the Vatican
because of his sister's escapade with one of the ecclesiastics.

Musically and intellectually Scarlatti was of the old school
and was steeped in classicism. He spent many years in Naples
(1683–1719) and his prolific outpouring of works literally
monopolized the stages there. He was so popular in that city
(and so favored by wealthy patronage) that he is accredited
with founding the Neapolitan school of opera. His eighty-eight
works for the theater were all composed in twenty-odd years.
As with all notoriously successful artists, he was the object of
countless imitators. His younger admirers made the serious
mistake of attempting to re-create not his best works but his
most successful ones.

Until Scarlatti appeared, overtures for operas had no recognizable form and had nothing to do with the action that was to
follow. The Neopolitan master devised his overture in three
distinct parts. The first section was quick-paced and light,
probably to perk the audience up and draw its attention to the
occasion. This was followed by a melodious, slower section,
and the overture was brought to its conclusion by way of an-

other vigorous, fast section. The Scarlatti overture has become known as the real Italian overture.

Early German composers and librettists were showing a minimum of daring in their choice of themes and ideas, due, no doubt, to the influence of the powerful Lutheran church. The Church saw absolutely nothing to admire in the sophisticated and immoral atmosphere of the new entertainment form. But religion had little control over the power of music, and before much time had passed, secular works—translated from the popular Italian and French theater successes—found a welcome home in the German repertory.

Opera madness was sweeping ahead, and every country that was introduced to her appeared unable to do anything but succumb. In a matter of years she was a glittering institution. Opera houses became the proud symbols of the greatness of cities. Opera singers became the sought-after, fought-over celebrities of the time. Opera was suddenly an international commodity.

CHAPTER TWO

Opera Seria, Opera Buffa, and the Singers

Composers of the seventeenth and eighteenth centuries were allowed little freedom. The laws regarding the creation of an opera were rigid and unrelentingly formal. No matter how original his aims, the poor composer was forced to conform to orthodox rules—even regarding the number of singers to be used in his work. Tradition had established that no more than three women and three men could be employed to interpret an opera. The composer was rarely allowed another singer, no matter how persistent his demands may have been. The prima donna (first woman) was generally a high soprano, the second preferably a contralto. More importantly, the *primo uomo* (first man) always had to be a *castrato*.

This unique and now extinct type of singer was the glory of a period of blazing vocal virtuosity. It was a time when Italian singing schools flourished and produced a breed of singer who often held more power than the political rulers of the day.

For many years the great Roman church choirs had used the talents of *castrati*, but as opera's popularity increased, and extremely florid, ornamented music became the vogue, these men, whose emasculation at the time of puberty allowed them to retain their soprano or alto singing sound, became greatly in demand.

It has been recorded that during the eighteenth century some four thousand boys were castrated throughout all Italy. It is safe to say that a very small number of these boys' parents —or they themselves—ever realized their dreams of success and glory.

As these *castrati* matured, the beautiful, high pitch of their voices remained. In addition, their lung capacity and power grew to immense proportions. The power and the unique castrato sound became the rage of the opera world. Some of their immense popularity with audiences and impresarios was also due to the scarcity of women singers during part of the seventeenth century. Also, for many years, women were not allowed to perform in public theaters. The *castrati* were excellent musicians. Most of them had been trained in the finest music schools since boyhood as part of the calculated parental preparation for illustrious careers. The most famous of all the *castrati* was Carlo Broschi, popularly known as *Farinelli*. He had a legendary career and included two kings of Spain among his devoted admirers.

Singers and composers were concerned with two, distinctive types of opera—*opera seria* (serious opera) and *opera buffa* (comic opera). Generally, singers specialized in one or the other, but occasionally the versatile performers participated in both.

The basis of eighteenth-century *opera seria* can be traced to the changes made in the seventeenth-century libretto. The poet Pietro Metastasio (1698–1782) is chiefly responsible for specific alterations that gave the operas of that time something more than a haphazard form. His librettos decreed that the drama and the music give way to each other in patterns of tension followed by release. In other words, the dramatic action was first explored in the *recitative* and then the leading singer-actor expressed his personal feelings and thoughts in an *aria,* an air or song of some complexity. Metastasio took great care and pleasure in placing these songs at the exactly right and most impressive part of the drama. Another of Metastasio's reforms was to cut away anything resembling the comic in his plots. He was convinced that humor was incompatible with tragedy.

Today, the conductor is the virtuoso, the power behind an opera performance, but in the eighteenth century the singer was king. He dominated everyone connected with the presentation of opera—even the composer. The singers' excesses of temperament and improvisation grew by leaps and bounds. Even Metastasio, who, by expanding the possibilities of the aria, had in a way released this new breed of destructive nightingale, could not correct the state of affairs. His cries that the singers were destroying his dramas fell on deaf ears. The public adored these exciting characters; the singer could do no wrong.

Comic opera eventually found its own independent format in a distinctly nationalistic style. It went its separate way in all the countries of Europe and displayed its entertainment wares in the language of the common people. Often it poked raucous fun at its austere and aristocratic sister *opera seria.* Her followers reacted with no sense of humor and considered this new form bawdy, circus entertainment. The country cousin had little to fear—barely a hundred years passed before comic opera had won complete domination of the musical theater.

At the start of the eighteenth century there were two types of *opera buffa* in Italy—comic, pastoral pieces and *intermezzi*. These short, one-act works were intended to be performed between the acts of a grander, more serious work. Literally hundreds of these *intermezzi* came into being, and one of them, Pergolesi's *La serva padrona* 1733 (*The Maid Mistress*), has retained its sparkling popularity into our present time. Folk melodies and patter songs for the bass voice made their first appearance in these frothy *intermezzi* whose music is notable for its sensitive awareness of the text. Whereas serious opera had been chiefly concerned with solo singing, comic opera branched out and developed the different ensemble forms. The ensemble sprang into importance when the composers wrote music for rollicking finales to these *intermezzi* that combined the voices of all the principal singers. Unable to resist the success of their comic competitors, serious musicians introduced the idea into *opera seria*.

This new-found form, however, with all its expression of freedom and lightheartedness, adhered to its own dogma. The arrangement of voices in *opera buffa* was just as rigid as that for *opera seria*. The composer had to write for two groups —the *buffo* division which was made up of two women and three men (the third was always a bass), and the subordinate group, inevitably two lovers who were exceedingly serious and romantic.

Eventually, *opera buffa* broke out of its own simple and limited mold and blossomed into more complicated, full-length works.

Domenico Cimarosa (1749–1801) was one of the most gifted writers of Italian comic opera in the late eighteenth century, and his *Il Matrimonio Segreto* (*The Secret Marriage*), a masterpiece of its kind that rivals both Mozart and Rossini, is one of more than eighty operas he composed in this manner.

Comic opera (*opéra comique*) in France began under the guidance of Molière and Lully. Their presentations—ballets combined with theater pieces consisting of songs and spoken dialogue—were created primarily to entertain Louis XIV. Their competition at that time seems to have been negligible. An Italian Theater in Paris was attempting to keep its head above water with performances of Italian farces of questionable taste—comedies to which they added ballets and songs. When the Italians were tossed out of Paris, their productions were quickly picked up by French groups, who if anything, did less about the quality and taste of their neighbors' artistic efforts. These "popular" theaters and their performers found themselves playing mostly during the fair weeks in Paris. The Fair Theaters, as they came to be known, eventually met with more success, and in 1715 the establishment of the Théâtre de L'Opéra-Comique afforded their burlesques a permanent home.

Due chiefly to the talents and integrity of André Grétry and Étienne Nicolas Méhul, the *comique* form that had begun as something far from original developed into one of the most respected and popular examples of French art. Grétry was a Belgian, who, after studying in Italy, settled in Paris in 1767. Parisians applauded some forty-odd comic operas of his. *Zémire et Azor* and *Richard Coeur de Lion* are two of his greatest successes.

As the years passed and the blood of the French Revolution flowed, *opéra comique* held its own. True, there was a dearth of composers who could begin to emulate the gifts and popularity of Grétry, but 1812 welcomed the return of one François Adrien Boieldieu and his tremendously popular *Jean de Paris*. *Opéra comique* was not dead.

Comic opera, across the channel in England, was another story. The English had absolutely no empathy or sympathy for their foreign cousins' style and ability to be amused in the area of *opera seria* or *opera buffa*. They retaliated nationalistically by creating their own comic opera. These ballad operas comically lampooned *opera seria* in a language and presentation that stuck close to the bawdy vernacular of the streets of London. John Gay's *The Beggar's Opera* (1728) extolled ladies of easy virtue, thieves, and anyone against the "establishment" of the day. Its satirical songs and dialogue, highlighted with its humorous defamation of Italian opera, regaled audiences for years. The public seemingly never tired of hearing its familiar ballad tunes—spiced with obvious bits of other composers' works—or story that had lived its raucous life for many years. It intrigued Kurt Weill in the twentieth century, and the famous German composer's wife, Lotte Lenya, assisted his version *The Threepenny Opera* to sensational success not only in Berlin but in New York City several years ago. Weill's version became one of the longest-running productions in New York, and its "hit" song, "Mack the Knife," made golden-record history for more than one singer, including Louis Armstrong.

Other ballad operas followed *The Beggar's Opera,* and their popularity telegraphed the death of Italian opera in England. But as the fickle public began to tire of the same old tunes, the composers—in a search to find a way of pleasing the crowd—took new courage. They began to interject their own original music into the scores. One was Dr. Thomas Arne (1710-1778) who was probably the most renowned composer of this time. His *Thomas and Sally* was tremendously successful and has managed to have many revivals. Its success was so encouraging that he introduced six of his own songs into his *Love in the Village,* a comic opera that utilized the compositions of some sixteen different composers.

Of the three most successful eighteenth-century composers of English comic opera—Thomas Linley, Sr., Charles Dibdin, and William Shield—Shield was the most talented and the most popular. In 1782, his *Rosina* showed an adventurous ability to move forward and forget the vaudevillian atmosphere of many ballad operas. Henry Rowley Bishop (1786–1855) proceeded in this direction in the nineteenth century. Contemporary audiences are not likely to hear any of his more than one hundred compositions—unless, that is, some prima donna nostalgically decides to render his "Lo, Here the Gentle Lark" or "Home Sweet Home," as they have been known to do, going so far as to interpolate one or the other into the lesson scene in Rossini's *Il Barbiere di Siviglia* (*The Barber of Seville*).

Quite obviously, the English during this period of comic opera did not make any grave change in the world of music. With typical British strength they held fast and remained as indomitable as the Cliffs of Dover in their refusal to swing around to anything that gave the slightest appearance of domination by a foreign music element. But, music and opera in England grew. One of England's glories was to be the comic genius of Gilbert and Sullivan; another, its opera house in Covent Garden. But, a German was about to visit them and make some changes.

CHAPTER THREE

Eighteenth-century Opera and the Amazing Mr. Handel

George Frederick Handel was born in Halle, Saxony. The year, 1685, was a year that also heralded the arrival of Johann Sebastian Bach. Handel's father, a well-to-do barber-surgeon, was sixty-three years old when George was born and had not during all his years shown even a tolerance for, much less an understanding of, anything musical. His second wife, George's mother, was a less-than-brilliant clergyman's daughter. For heredity to have had its way it would seem likely that the Handels' son should have followed in their amazingly nonartistic footsteps. But fate had it otherwise. George quite mysteriously learned to play the organ and the clavier.

Often, while he was in Grammar School, he went with his father to visit the Duke of Saxe-Weissenfels. The elderly gentleman overheard the boy playing the chapel organ and insisted that the elder Handel attend to his gifted son's musical education. Being something of a wordly business man, Papa Handel was not one to ignore a suggestion from a titled nobleman. Young Handel's music lessons with the organist of the

Liebfrauenkirche in Halle began immediately. In three years he had taught the young genius all he knew of harmony, counterpoint, the harpsichord, violin, and oboe. He had also introduced George to the intoxicating sounds of Italian music. At eleven, George made a visit to the sophisticated royal court at Berlin. Although he made the journey alone, it must be assumed that the clever boy made immediate and important contacts, and soon he was playing a command performance before the Electress Sophia Charlotte and her entourage. His virtuosity so impressed the Princess that she proposed sending him to Italy for work with the great musicians of the time. Perhaps news traveled more rapidly than one imagines in the seventeenth century, because the elder Handel heard of the royal suggestion and ordered his son to return home at once. En route, the boy heard that his father had died. Being a dutiful son, he finished his preparatory studies and entered the university to study law. Music, however, was a gnawing and persistent force that he could not ignore. In 1702 he took a temporary job as the Domkirche's organist. Considering the fact that he was only seventeen and also that he was not of the Domkirche's Calvinist religion, it can be surmised that his being given such an important position had a great deal to do with his extraordinary and recognizable talent.

He was recognized not only by the Domkirche group; he was heard by the famous and prolific composer Georg Philipp Telemann, who openly praised him. A year later, the young Handel responded to the call of greener challenges and left for Hamburg.

Hamburg, a seaport city, was the citadel of German opera, and its artistic commandant was Reinhard Keiser (1674-1739).

Keiser must be included in the group of early eighteenth-century composers whose operatic work, while staying within the long-established framework, gave us some of the finest dramatic music of the time. Keiser is said to have composed more than 120 operas. He was a facile and secure writer, and much of his work is more than a little reminiscent—to researchers—of Mozart. It is regrettable that an artist of such talent and power should also be the one to whom the finger points when any discussion involves the decline and possible death of a true German opera. His later operas and their librettos show an obvious attention to "playing down" to the public appetites—they are full of vulgarities and attempts to please mass tastes.

Not long after young George's arrival in Hamburg, he was playing the violin and harpsichord in Keiser's theater. At the opera house, George met the composer Johann Mattheson. Mattheson had also been a law student, and he and Handel had much in common. Not to be overlooked is that Johann was a singer and he often conducted. In addition he had had one of his own operas produced and he assisted Handel in increasing his knowledge of the manifold complexities and involvements of Hamburg's great opera house.

George seems to have been little affected by the open freedom and notoriously liberal atmosphere of Hamburg. He quietly and diligently perfected his music and tried to keep his friendship with Mattheson alive. This posed some difficulties because Mattheson's vain demands and his envy of Handel's obviously superior talent often erupted into open arguments. Upon one occasion, a duel followed a performance of Mattheson's opera *Cleopatra*. The work had been a spectacular success —one that elevated Mattheson to the position of a public idol.

He had not only written it, he also performed the leading role of Antony. Then, when the noble Roman died, he returned to the pit to take the conductor's position at the clavier. Handel was the conductor for these performances, and a strong-willed one at that. At one of the repetitions he refused to remove himself from the clavier when Mattheson entered the pit. The angry words and blows that resulted culminated in a challenge to draw swords after the final curtain had come down. The story goes—and the opera world is blessed for it—that Johann's sword broke on one of George's buttons. The drama of the moment was lost and the duel was over. With youthful adaptability they patched things up, and in a few weeks they were both rehearsing Handel's first opera, in which Mattheson was the leading tenor. It was called *Almira*. His second opera, *Nero,* was hardly the sensational success that *Almira* had been, but the attention being paid this new, young composer angered the all-powerful Kaiser who, illogically and stupidly, made life in Hamburg intolerable for Handel. In 1706 George left for Italy.

He spent some time in Florence and then traveled on to Rome. Opera in the Eternal City was having a bad time. The Pope had put a ban on performances, and there was no immediate sign of its being lifted. Handel returned to Florence where his opera *Rodrigo* was presented under the auspices of Ferdinand de' Medici. With its success as proof that he had a command of the Italian singing style, Handel was eager to head for Venice and test himself.

Venice's fifteen opera houses reacted with blunt coolness and refused to stage his works. Despite the attitude of the theaters, Handel was recognized by the musicians of Venice—namely Domenico Scarlatti, son of Alessandro. Their friendship, one that endured for many years, began at a costume ball. After hearing the virtuoso harpsichord performance of the masked Handel, Scarlatti shouted, "That must either be the famous Saxon or the Devil himself."

Handel went back to Rome—this time with Scarlatti. The success of his *Rodrigo* had alerted the Holy City, and he was greeted with attention from everyone of any importance.

The clever Romans and the no less clever Handel quickly found a solution to the papal ban. George composed *La Risurrezione (The Resurrection)*. It was actually an opera in the acceptable disguise of an oratorio. Handel became the topic of conversation in musical Rome, and eventually he wrote another oratorio. This one was enhanced by the patronage of a nephew of the Pope, Cardinal Ottobuoni. Unfortunately, his patronage and the performance of the musicians did not enhance *Il Trionfo del Tempo e del Disinganno (The Triumph of Time and Design)* enough to make it a success. It was a failure.

Next he visited Naples but little came of his year's stay there, except the importance of his meeting with the Imperial Viceroy, Cardinal Grimani. This educated and cultured Venetian was responsible for the libretto of Handel's next opera, *Agrippina*.

His new opera was a spectacular success and played before packed houses in the Teatro San Giovanni Crisostomo for twenty-seven performances. It was his best to date and includes one of his finest overtures. The overture to an opera or oratorio is an orchestral piece that precedes the major work. It generally alludes to what will take place in the opera.

Agrippina's overture is in the French style, as were most

Handelian overtures. They reflect the influence of Jean-Phi-lippe Rameau (1683–1764). Rameau's reputation as an organ-ist and composer of harpsichord music was well established years before Parisians had heard his lyric tragedy, *Hippolyte et Aricie,* in 1733. Two other notable works, *Castor et Pollux* and *Les Indes galantes* (*Gallant India*) are still performed today.

The adoring applause was ringing in Mr. Handel's ears, and *Agrippina* had made him an international success. His avid public treated him with more admiration than they did the powerful Doges. His ambitions to conquer musical Italy had far exceeded his hopes. He was undecided as to what to do next. Prince Ernst Augustus of Hanover was insistent that he accept a position at his brother's court. He no sooner became Kapellmeister of the Hanover opera house when he took a leave of absence and went to England. Kapellmeister is Ger-man for chapelmaster. Originally the word signified the music director of a nobleman's private chapel. Later the term was used for the resident conductor of an orchestra.

Without knowing a word of the English language, Handel arrived in a country that was hardly responsive to foreign com-posers, and conditions musically were as gray as the fog that hung over the Thames. The great English composer Henry Purcell had died just fifteen years before Handel's arrival, and English music and musicians had done little to show any signs of going beyond him, let alone replacing him. Purcell's only opera, *Dido and Aeneas,* is a gem of perfection, and Handel was to learn much from his music. He not only learned from it; he borrowed whatever appealed to him. What we have come to think of as Handel's English style, particularly in his monumental choruses, has a distinct air of Purcell about it.

Now Handel was in enemy territory. He was in London where the society of the day held great affection for Italian opera, although not a single opera company had been able really to establish itself. There were singers by the score—but no composers of any consequence to write for them. Also, the theaters of the day were located in a part of town that would have made Mack the Knife feel at home. The lords and ladies demanded something more enticing than a mediocre opera to get them to take their lives in their hands to hear it.

The gods continued to smile on George. When Queen Anne died (1714), the same Prince of Hanover who had encouraged the composer in Germany was crowned George I of England. The following year, as a reward for the success of his opera, *Amadigi,* the new king appointed Handel music master for the royal princesses—a position that carried with it a sizable yearly pension.

Serse (*Xerxes*) was Handel's only attempt at comic opera. It is rarely performed today and remembered by thousands only because of its tenor aria—*"Ombra mai fù"* ("There was never such a shade").

Handel's career as a wildly acclaimed opera composer was finished in 1741. His sight was failing him and he was bankrupt.

He was not one to give up at the age of fifty-six, and he turned to the oratorio field. Although he wrote several oratorios during his lifetime, none equaled the enduring success of his majestic *Messiah*. It was written in the miraculously short period of three weeks and had its first performance in Dublin in 1742. At its first London performance, the king, George II, stood up during the singing of the moving "Hallelujah." It was a spontaneous reaction to the spiritual beauty of the music. Quite naturally, the audience followed the king's move. This custom of standing during the final section is adhered to in performances all over the world today.

The death of Italian opera in England seemed to have no reaction on the rest of the world. Opera grew and attracted composers of all nationalities. The Italian school and its disciples still had much to say and the determination to say it.

The French school, confined to Paris, was not aware that an Austrian-Czech was about to break its rigid bonds. His reforms would leave an indelible imprint on the history of all opera.

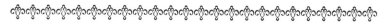

CHAPTER FOUR

Gluck and the Time for Change

Christoph Willibald Gluck (1714-1787) was born in Germany. The family moved to Vienna when Gluck's father took a position as gamekeeper to the royal house of Prince Lobkowitz. At eighteen, after a preliminary education that was apparently not overloaded with music, Christoph went to Prague. Evidently that city and the Czechoslovakians were an inspiration because the real Gluck—the musician—was reborn there. Music became his life.

Prince Lobkowitz' generosity was inherited by his son and the younger Prince asked Christoph to return to Vienna as one of his private musicians.

Connections and contracts were as important on the Ringstrasse in 1735 as they are on Madison Avenue today. Lobkowitz introduced Gluck to another prince, a Milanese named Melzi. This introduction would eventually change the world of opera.

Melzi convinced Gluck that he must go to Italy. And he did. Four years later, Gluck's first opera, *Artaserse*, was produced. His librettist was the popular Metastasio. The success of *Arta-*

serse made Gluck much in demand, and London's Haymarket Theatre beckoned. Now Gluck was drawn into the celebrated circle of Handel, who was in command of his own Italian theater.

The egotistical and outspoken Handel is known to have said: "Gluck doesn't know as much about counterpoint as my cook." Actually, Handel's cook—who was also his valet—was a first-class musician. Luckily, the opinion did not destroy the younger composer and he gained considerably from their relationship.

Gluck was aware that Italian opera was showing signs of deterioration. To him, the reasons were obvious. The words had no dramatic importance, and most Italian operas were blatant singing contests—contests that often developed into onstage battles between rival "stars." Although these virtuoso performances were packing the theaters, Gluck could see that opera itself had slipped into a position very close to the brink of unimaginative mediocrity.

Opera performances had by this time become merely another opportunity for society to show off its jewels and clothes and indulge in the latest gossip. During these performances the raucous laughter accompanying the latest bit of scandal and the clang of dishes and glasses often outdistanced the golden, pear-shaped tones of the artists on stage. In many opera houses the wealthy patrons took it as a matter of course that a pleasant supper and an abundance of wine should be served during the performance. After all, why should one give all his attention to the stage and the people on it when business of the day was of more importance. Hadn't the subscribers already heard many of the melodies—even in their reworked newer versions of virtuosity?

Occasionally some of Jean Baptiste Lully's operas diverted the patrons from a cool game of dice or a heated political conversation—if only to watch the stage mechanics. The plot and the music may have been old hat, but audiences "bravoed" the graphic pictures of a city going up in flames or a town demolished by a fake, lava-spewing volcano, or the sparkling jets of a magnificent fountain. The plot may have been a bore, but the scenic action was compelling. Perhaps the French were right. Today's audiences listen to Lully's music as something of a museum memory—a return to the era of Louis XV.

Gluck was certainly conscious of the state of affairs, but it appears that he did not give it his undivided attention until after his stint, which was unsuccessful, in London. Actually, his lack of success in England was his own failing. He was not an inspired creator of Italian opera—whether its days were numbered or not. Gluck had been only too willing to whip up pale imitations of some of Johann Adolf Hasse's popular operas which he had first heard in Prague.

For the fifteen years that followed his depressing disappointment in London, Gluck gave his friends and his admirers at the Viennese court the impression he was continuing to function within his usual imitative framework. The impression was inaccurate. What he was actually doing was studying avidly and preparing himself for a revolution—an operatic one.

In 1750 he married Marianna Pergin. She was plain, to say the least, but she did bring her husband a sizable dowry that afforded him the privilege of never being pressured by the demands of making a living. This was definitely a proper state for a composer of his ideas and plans.

While Gluck was enjoying life—and allowing his reformation plans time to ferment—he reached the decision that Metastasio's librettos were no longer functional. Their plots and characters were out of focus and stilted. Fortunately Gluck was introduced to a freewheeling poet, Raniero da Calzabigi, who had lived for many years in Paris and had—when not involved in numerous love affairs—acquired an admirable understanding of the French style. Calzabigi's libretto for *Orfeo ed Euridice* was more than good drama; it was a perfect text for Gluck and his idea that the words and the music must be a perfect entity.

The Orpheus myth had been used before—but never in this way. The tale of a singer, Orpheus, whose life has been shattered by the death of his wife, Euridice, and how the gods allow the youth to bring her back from the Elysian Fields—on the condition that he not look back at her until they both reached the real world—is an enduring masterpiece.

Calzabigi broke out of the confinements of the original legend and added a bright, happy ending. Amor, a goddess, restores Euridice's life, and the lovers are reunited.

Gluck was wise and extremely subtle in the handling of his cast of three principals. Each character becomes a living person through his music. Also the music urges the story along with delicately shaded nuances for every changing dramatic scene. *Orfeo* didn't alter the direction of opera as instantaneously as some would have us believe. At its premiere (sung in Italian) in Vienna the role of Orpheus was sung by a *castrato*. The public greeted the opera with cool disdain, and it took the work more than a year to catch on. When it did, the accompanying money and success enabled Gluck to move into a sumptuous villa where he proceeded to instruct the young ladies of the court in the art of singing. One of them was Marie Antoinette. He also slipped back into his lazy, stereotyped style of writing.

Gluck's second new-style opera, *Alceste,* was accepted with the same initial response that had greeted *Orfeo*—cool Viennese detachment and annoyance. His composer-colleagues waspishly attacked Gluck for attacking their works of art, and the spoiled and volatile singers wept in dismay when they found that Gluck's music gave them no opportunities for vocal displays.

His third opera, *Paride ed Elena* (*Paris and Helen*), fared no better. Gluck openly defied the public and his supposed patrons, at the same time scoring them for their lack of imagination. The attitude of the Viennese hurt him deeply and he decided to exchange the chestnut blossoms of Vienna for those in Paris. There, he lashed out at the deplorable opera choruses which wore masks while singing and never used a single gesture; and particularly at the orchestra members who did not know the difference between *crescendo* and *diminuendo,* and wore gloves to keep their hands clean—while they were playing!

Through the political sleight of hand of a friend and his own rapport with Marie Antoinette, who was now a Dauphine (and a lady of no mean influence in Paris), his *Iphigénie en Aulide* was performed in 1774. Despite the heroic antagonism of his enemies in the Italian opera camp, *Iphigénie* was a triumph.

At long last—at sixty—Gluck became the most celebrated composer in Europe. For the duration of his career, Gluck was quick to respond to rivalry. His greatest achievements were the result of his greatest challenges. One was his last great success, *Iphigénie en Tauride.*

The public, the press, and the nobility of France had taken sides for and against him. His adversary was Nicola Piccini (1728–1800). The two composers were given the same story and asked to set it to music. It was a traumatic and embarrassing situation that was coldly devised to destroy either one or the other of them. A touch of pathos was added by the fact that the two men were friends.

Gluck's opera was the winner. The year was 1779.

Musically it is possible that Gluck was not that much greater than several of his long-overlooked contemporaries. That he is the so-called "father of modern opera" is because of what he did with the finest parts of German, Italian, and French opera. To do this he had to take, discard, and add. His operatic reforms were based on the demands of a group of knowledgeable writers who knew and understood music. They were known as the Encyclopedists. They condemned French opera as "spectacle where the whole happiness and misery of people consists in seeing dancing about them," and for the fact that "the characters in opera never say what they ought to. They speak in maxims and proverbs. When each has sung two or three couplets, the scene is ended, and the dancing begins anew; if it did not we should die of boredom."

Basically they were demanding:

1. Changes in the performing styles of opera, including the acting, the singing, and the instrumental performances.

2. Drastic changes in librettos.

3. Changes in the music drama.

Gluck was certainly their man for not only did he believe that "simplicity, truth, and naturalness are the great fundamentals of beauty in the production of all art," he wrote music for the theater. When his music was criticized—and it often was —he would question the critic: "Did it displease you in the theater? No? Well, then, that is enough. When I have got my effect in the theater, I have got all I wanted: it matters very little if my music is not agreeable in the concert hall."

Gluck returned to Vienna in 1779. Miserable and suffering from a stroke, he composed little in his last years. For the most part he and his wife lived a financially secure but lonely life.

At seventy-three, when Gluck died, his ideas had carried classic music and classic tragedy to an utterly beautiful, very cerebral, and strangely withdrawn mountaintop. He wanted to write music for which time and popular fashion were nonexistent. Even beyond that he wanted to write music which, in his own words, "will eliminate the ridiculous distinctions between music of different nations."

CHAPTER FIVE

Singspiel and the Incredible Mozart

The baroque, picture-postcard city of Salzburg makes an ideal setting for the birthplace of a genius. It is on the sunlit route that leads from Venice to Vienna—two undisputed capitals of opera—and its atmosphere glitters with rococo sophistication and smiles with the eyes of eternal childhood.

Wolfgang Amadeus Mozart (1756–1791) was born there. He was one of seven children born to Leopold Mozart and his beautiful wife. Five of their children died at a very early age and the determination that the two survivors, Nannerl and Wolfgang, should live brilliant and memorable lives became an obsession with their father.

At eight, Nannerl had already shown signs of becoming an impressive clavier performer. Wolfgang, at three, wasn't far behind. At five, after a year of lessons, he was composing. When Wolfgang was six, his father decided that the time was ripe to display his *wunderkinder* to the world. He was right.

Munich, in 1762, took the precocious performers to her heart —especially Wolfgang. That same year the Mozarts traveled to Vienna where they became the toast of the town. They had scarcely settled in their rooms when they were invited to play a command performance before the gilded court of Maria Theresa.

In addition to his precocity, Wolfgang was blessed with an abundant, effusive, and winning charm. The court found his insistent and open questions (even to the Empress)—"Do you love me? Do you really love me?"—irresistible. And, agreeing with their ruler, they could only answer, "Yes."

The great homes of Vienna opened their doors and vied with one another in lavish offerings of their affection and adoration. Unfortunately, Wolfgang was suddenly deprived of all this socializing; he was stricken with scarlet fever. As fate would have it, absence didn't make the Viennese hearts grow fonder, and by the time he was well, the fickle music set had lost interest in him.

The Mozarts, with some of the wind taken out of their sails, returned to Salzburg to plan a new attack.

Leopold's next palace-storming tour was greeted with so much acclaim they had no trouble at all in capturing the hearts and the patronage of the court of Versailles. Even the powerful and hesitant-to-succumb Madame de Pompadour had to give way to Wolfgang's radiant charm and talent.

Leopold was a man who knew a triumph when he smelled it. And he knew how to fan the flames of idolatry. He had four of his son's violin and clavier sonatas published with the dedication to one of the King's daughters. The move was a gem of musical politics.

The royal court of George III and Queen Charlotte in London also followed suit. The publicity of their successes on the continent—and with the English royal family—guaranteed that the children's first concert would be a spectacular success. It certainly was musically—and even more so when the box-office receipts were counted.

As the years went by, time took its toll, and Leopold, quick to realize that sixteen-year-old Nannerl was no longer a money-making child, turned all of his attentions to his eleven-year-old son. Although brother and sister had shared the billing throughout innumerable tours, it was obvious that Wolfgang was the natural "star."

When the family returned to Vienna both Nannerl and Wolfgang became victims of the serious smallpox epidemic that had taken over the city. The boy was blind for several days. Eventually he bounced back to health, as did Nannerl, and his parents were able to continue with their elaborate hopes for their son's career. They openly showed their disappointment that Wolfgang's illness had upset their plans to marry him off to a member of the royal family.

Mozart's first two operas, *La finta semplice* (*The Pretended Simpleton*) and *Bastien und Bastienne,* are products of these days in Vienna.

As obsessed as Leopold was for fame and fortune (by way of his genius son), he did realize that there must be time for rest. A year of rest in Salzburg meant hours of composing and practicing for the boy while papa was arranging a detailed tour of Italy, this time without Mrs. Mozart and Nannerl.

This next tour consisted of one success after another. It led them to Milan and the welcome patronage of its governor-general and the accolades of Gluck's celebrated teacher, Sammartini. The Bologna Philharmonic Society also made him a member of their august organization. It was difficult to believe that Wolfgang was just fourteen!

Holy Week found them in Rome. The story is that the boy, after hearing one performance of Allegri's renowned *Miserere,* was able to return to his rooms and write down all the nine parts and its two choruses. It was not only a feat of memorization; it almost got him excommunicated. After two years of arduous touring and performing, Wolfgang and his father returned to Salzburg. Commissions for an opera and an oratorio, plus a request for a work to be performed at the wedding of one of the many children of the Empress of Austria occupied his time for several months—then he returned to Italy. Back again in Salzburg, the young composer was confronted by the death of his old and wise patron, the archbishop of that city. His successor, a tyrant by the name of Hieronymus von Colloredo, Bishop of Gurk, remains to this day a villainous character equal to the best in fiction. When the news of his appointment reached the poor citizens of Salzburg, they were so heartsick they went into mourning.

A series of events during von Colloredo's discouraging reign led to the Mozarts' packing their bags once more and departing for more tolerable territory. To mention just a few: Wolfgang's opera *Il sogno di Scipione* (*The Dream of Scipio*), written for the Archbishop as a part of services celebrating any archbishop's being elevated to such an exalted position was a miserable disaster. We will only mention its name. Also, Wolfgang was made to wear servant's clothes, as well as to eat with the servants, and the devout tyrant often slapped him in anger. These reasons, plus that fact that his salary while working for the Bishop amounted to something like $225 for a whole year, hardly inspired him. The situation was even less encouraging for an ambitious genius who had become accustomed to more than a fair amount of elegance and adoration. In 1774 he received a commission from the opera in Munich. *La finta giardiniera* (*The Pretended Gardner*) pleased its audience, but nothing came of it. Back at home base, in Salzburg, he wrote *Il rè pastore* (*The Shepherd King*), a reasonably dull opera, whose aria *"L'amerò, sarò costante"* ("I will love patiently") still finds its way to the concert programs of contemporary sopranos.

By 1775 it became apparent to all who were interested in Mozart as a child prodigy and to those deeply concerned with his fulfillment as a mature musician that he and his music were going through a period of transition. Up to that time, his elegant, graceful, and lively works had been looked on with unqualified amazement mainly because he was, after all, a boy and a genius. Their brilliance was colored with eager self-confidence and mimicry of composers who had preceded him. Mozart's early music is more than clever, as many superficial critics claim it to be. It is music created by a youth touched with genius. Wolfgang was growing up and breaking away from the parental guidance and gratuities he no longer needed. The time graciously arrived when Leopold could no longer manipulate tours and concert appearances for his child side-show attraction; the boy had grown into a man.

Leaving childhood behind, particularly the childhood of a uniquely gifted musician, is a dangerous turn. Mozart the man was confronted with these dangers as he approached nineteen. His patrons and admirers were also concerned. They had been eager to believe in his genius when its technical virtuosity brightened their lives, especially when it was backed up with an exceedingly pretty, childish face and a winning smile. As he grew up, Mozart lost many of his attractive physical attributes and turned into a rather ordinary looking young man. Mozart was aware that early maturity had not enhanced his physical charm, and he began to compensate. At nineteen he was wearing elaborate coats, too much jewelry, and spending hours before the mirror dressing his hair. His growing up was not helped much by the dour Archbishop of Salzburg. All that Mozart wanted to do was compose operas, and the old man would not permit him to do so. In a letter written February 2, 1778, Mozart commented: "I am jealous of anyone who writes an opera. Tears come to my eyes when I hear an operatic air. . . ."

The boy felt that it was imperative that he travel again to more rewarding horizons. This time father was left behind.

In Manneheim he met his supposed wife-to-be. At the opera house he was introduced to Fridolin Weber, a prompter at the theater. A prompter is usually an assistant conductor of an opera house. He cues the singers during a performance and generally is seated in the prompter's "box"—at the front of the stage—and invisible to the audience. Some operas require the services of several prompters. And when a singer is ill-prepared, many an aria has become an audible duet—much to the amusement or dismay of the audience.

Weber invited young Mozart and his mother into his home. He had a family of several daughters, and it was not long before Wolfgang was hopelessly enamored of one of them, Aloysia. His romantic mind, one that had never overlooked the charms of attractive women, immediately turned his thoughts to marrying Fräulein Weber and, since she was a singer, taking her on a tumultuous tour of Italy as a concert performer. It is said that Wolfgang had never argued with nor disobeyed his father. Nor did he this time when Leopold got wind of the impending marriage plans. He ordered his son to get on to Paris. Wolfgang obeyed.

His arrival in Paris was hardly remarkable. The former child star was almost completely ignored. All that the glamourous Marie Antoinette could muster up for him was a starvation-wage position as an organist at Versailles. There was additional heartbreak when his mother died.

He deliberately delayed his return to Salzburg long enough to conduct in Manneheim and to visit Munich where he discovered that his romantic dream, Aloysia, had literally forgotten all about him.

During the next two years Mozart became more and more frustrated. In 1781 his first major opera was given a production during carnival time in Munich. Mozart had learned well from the operas of Gluck—so well that *Idomeneo* might have made the old reformer wonder if all his heartaches and strivings had been worth it. Mozart was willing to let the drama stop dead in its tracks while his musical ideas—and his singers—took flight in brilliant bravura. *Idomeneo* was always one of its composer's favorite operas. It was only mildly successful with the public.

By 1781 things were looking up for him; he was teaching, some of his music was published, and concert halls were once again demanding his performances. He also married Aloysia's younger sister, Constanze.

Just a year before their marriage, Mozart had begun work on his *Die Entführung aus dem Serail* (*The Abduction from the Seraglio*). Its libretto, full of comedy and fake Turkishisms, was clumsy and difficult for Mozart to work with. What he thought would be completed in a few months took almost a year.

Its premiere at the National Theater in Vienna was an unqualified success, and the audience demanded many encores. Mozart had given the music world the first major *singspiel,* or song-play. And to add to its importance, the work was the creation of a first-rate theater composer.

Through Mozart the *singspiel* reached a level of importance not thought possible. In common with all of Europe, Germany's sacred plays, with their similarity to the pastorals, miracle plays, and morality plays of other countries, had played an important part in the entertainment life of the people. But the *singspiel* used a secular plot. Since the songs had no recitative to connect them, and the performers spoke their dialogue and made their oftentimes crude jokes without the assistance of orchestral accompaniment, they were a far cry from opera.

The nobility may have derived pleasure from their beloved Italian opera, but the people held fast to their down-to-earth little plays with music. True, these *singspiels* that had sprung from the early German miracle plays got out of hand and degenerated into ribald obscenities, but Hans Sachs, a philosopher-cobbler in real life and also the leading character in Wagner's *Die Meistersinger von Nürnberg* (*The Mastersingers of Nuremburg*), is given credit for reforming this type of entertainment and setting it on the right road back to a worthwhile theatrical form.

Complications arise when one tries to draw a distinct line between opera and *singspiel*. In some song-plays the music is obviously second in importance to the other goings-on; in others the music definitely aims to develop the characters on stage—thus, these sections immediately acquire some of the dignity and eloquence of opera. But, once the composer's music even begins to aid and develop the dramatic fulfillment of the plot, we are confronted with opera, and *singspiel* is left in a class by itself.

Performances of *opera buffa* in Italy made a strong impression on Mozart during his many hectic tours of that country. Their comic, oftentimes burlesqued characters were to him truthful musical portraits of people. He was convinced that comedy was closer to mankind than vapid stories about antique gods and goddesses; it was impossible to communicate heavenly problems to audiences of his time. Evidently he was in touch with the times for three of the finest examples of *opera buffa* are from his imagination and pen: *Le Nozze di Figaro* (*The Marriage of Figaro*), *Don Giovanni,* and *Così fan tutte.*

After writing *Der Schauspieldirektor* (*The Impresario*), consisting of unfunny trivia about one Herr Buff and his problems with a troupe of singers, Lorenzo da Ponte—who had become Metastasio's successor as the giant of librettists—came to Mozart with the proposal that he write an opera using Beaumarchais' *Le Mariage de Figaro* for its plot.

Joseph II had banned all performances of the play because it was rife with provocative and political situations. Da Ponte was not about to be held back by a mere court ban, and he cleverly convinced the Emperor that the play could easily be produced as an opera *if* he were to cut away and clean up all of its feared political spots. With the Emperor's sanction he dashed off one of the greatest librettos that Mozart was ever to use. While working on the *Figaro* project, Mozart was also writing several extraordinary piano concertos—in order to pay the rent. The opera was completed in April, 1786, and performed for the first time on May 1. Screams of approval were heard from every seat in the theater and shouts of "Live, live, great Mozart!" greeted every encore of the work.

Beaumarchais was born in France just prior to the Revolution, and his plays, especially *The Barber of Seville* and *The Marriage of Figaro,* preached dangerous themes for those times. He rose from poverty to great wealth and by adding the *de* to his name attracted the patronization of the very same powdered-wig upper class whose shortsighted vision did not allow them to see that a Beaumarchais play had more than a little part in trundling them off to the Place de Guillotine.

Mozart, with memories of days he had suffered under the brutal inequalities of the rule of the Bishop of Salzburg, was certainly one to satirize the situation musically!

Beaumarchais rose to dizzy heights of popularity in Paris. He also became a familiar face in the prisons there. Later he brought guns from Holland to support the French Revolution. Some twenty years before that bloody time, the Americans must surely have been grateful to him—he had sold guns and ammunition to the colonists for their Revolution.

The rollicking beauty of *The Marriage of Figaro* begins with the overture and sings, dances, and spins its way through songs, recitatives, small choruses, and a finale that entwines the voices of seven singers. In this finale, each singer is individually characterized with loving care.

Although the Emperor was lavish in his praise of *Figaro*—as was the public at every performance—no permanent form of income was forthcoming from the court. Mozart and his family quickly spent the amount of money he had received for his masterpiece, so an invitation from Prague to oversee the Czech production of *Figaro* was accepted. When he walked into the opera house, there was an ovation that must have gladdened his heart. Later when he conducted the work himself, he was the recipient of praise and glory that he had not experienced since his childhood days. His every wish was a command, and he returned to Vienna with a commission to write an opera for the people of Prague.

Da Ponte was his librettist again. He turned to a one-act opera by Gazzaniga and Bertati called *Il Convitato di Pietra* (*The Stone Guest*) which was still another version of the famous Don Juan legend.

The well known lover, Don Juan, had been the subject for many poets and playwrights but none of them had seemingly settled on a completely acceptable way of ending his life. Mozart and Da Ponte came to the conclusion that the best idea was to have the entire cast, that is, all those who had not died or been killed in the action, join in a finale that sang of the moral of the play. This moralizing was often used in French *opéra comique*.

The overture is certainly not Mozart at his scintillating best but its first measures establish immediately the two forces that are the backbone of the drama itself. The first is the selfish, amoral, human drive of Don Juan, and the second is the Don's fight against some mysterious, godlike superpower.

In Italian Don Juan becomes Don Giovanni, and the title role is sung by a bass or baritone voice. And the touching and comic role of the Don's servant, Leporello, is also sung by a bass. Of the many services that Mozart did for opera, one that certainly should be remembered is that he was the first composer to demonstrate how thrilling the bass voice could be.

Don Giovanni offers both of its bass characters some of the opera's most rewarding music to sing. Notably, Leporello's famous catalogue aria, *Madamina! il catalogo* ("My dear lady, here is the catalog"), in which the servant energetically informs one of the Don's former ladyloves, Donna Elvira, that his master has a notorious list of amours in every country in Europe. Giovanni's champagne aria and the tender Don-Zerlina duet, *Là ci darem la mano* ("Your hand is in mine, dear one"), are also good examples of Mozart's ability to write for the bass voice that up to this time had been too much ignored.

Joseph II asked Mozart and Da Ponte to write another opera. They obliged him with *Così fan tutte*. This rococo and frivolous comic opera's title is translated as *They All Do It* or *The School for Lovers,* and it is a real Italian *opera buffa* with nothing more serious on its mind than telling the story of how two young men decide to put their girl friends to the test of fidelity. *Così fan tutte* had its first performance at the Burgtheater in Vienna, and amazingly enough it was not heard in the United States until 1922. Even more amazing is that European audiences, especially the Viennese, found it delightfully shock-

ing. To Hollywood- and television-indoctrinated audiences of
our time there is neither a line of dialogue nor a situation that
could cause even a mild blush.

If Mozart's spirits were bolstered to a new high with the success of *Così,* they were dashed to a new low with the death of
his benefactor, Joseph II, three weeks after the premiere. Leopold II, who followed Joseph to the throne, was a horse of another color. Not only did he care little for music, he cared less
for Mozart.

Unhappy and ill, Mozart was asked to write an opera for the
festivities to honor the coronation of Leopold II as King of
Bohemia. His need of money and sheer will power somehow
miraculously made it possible for him to finish *La Clemenza di
Tito* in two months' time. The Bohemian Queen rewarded
him by calling it "Rubbish!" A fine overture and memorable
aria for the soprano are hardly enough to keep it alive today.

Prague, the city of earlier triumphs, was in a different mood
after the failure of this *opera seria,* and Mozart went back to
Vienna even more unhappy and definitely not improved in
health.

He began to work again on *Die Zauberflöte* (*The Magic
Flute*) which he had started in 1791 at the request of an old
friend, the actor-manager Emanuel Schikaneder. They had
known each other during Mozart's Salzburg period, and Schikaneder quickly convinced Mozart that he should write the
music for a batch of his ideas. These ideas ran the gamut of
opera seria, opera buffa, earthy comedy, mysticism, and no small
amount of Freemasonry. And, in addition, the *singspiel* was to
include a fine role for Schikaneder.

Again one of the opera's leading characters, Sarastro, is a bass. His majestic arias, *"O Isis und Osiris"* and *"In diesen heil'gen Hallen"* ("Within This Hallowed Dwelling"), are impressive for their noble melody and deeply moving serenity. On the other hand, two arias for the evil Queen of the Night are fiendishly difficult coloratura arias whose blazing vocal displays have lured more than one courageous soprano into stratospheric places she should have considered more seriously before entering. The story of this fairy tale "mystery play," with its bird-people, Egyptians, a frustrated Queen of the Night and her beautiful daughter, trials by fire and water, is better left to a gifted storyteller. It really cannot be condensed—nor can all the complications that involved Mozart and his wily collaborator.

Complicated or not, the Viennese took the music and the story to their hearts, and it was one of Mozart's supreme triumphs. There were many, no doubt even then, who realized what Mozart had achieved. He had elevated the *singspiel* to its very highest possible form.

What they did not know was that *he,* by creating a thoroughly new theater-music language, was responsible for the future of German opera. He had opened the door for Beethoven, Weber, and Wagner.

Also, and just as important, all his operas, including *The Magic Flute* added a new conception to the accepted traditional forms. We must not forget that the term "originality" was never considered important or even something to be sought after by baroque composers. Originality came into its own only in the romantic periods of the nineteenth and twentieth centuries. Mozart was not a great original either, but as Donald Jay Grout has brought to our attention in his *A Short History of the Opera*: "His characters are viewed from the point which most strongly emphasizes their individuality, namely their love relationships. No composer has ever sung of human love in such manifold aspects or with such psychological penetration; and in every instance it is the *person,* not the abstract emotion, that is central. When finally, as in *The Magic Flute,* sexual love is subordinated to a mystic ideal and the individual begins to be a symbol as well as a person, we may feel that a path has been opened which will ultimately lead to the music drama of Wagner."

Mozart's contemporaries complained that he could not write for the voice. Time has proved them wrong, of course. There are singers and teachers of singing today who believe that if one can sing Mozart, one can sing anything. He himself carefully planned his arias for singers and said, "I like an aria to fit the singer as perfectly as a well-made suit of clothes."

There are those who contend that the boy who was born into a porcelain, rose-colored rococo atmosphere had only his times to thank for all his bubbling, gay, and fun-provoking music. This is far from the truth, for Mozart lived and experienced a time that was full of tension and despair for all the Western world. As adored as he was—at the times when the glittering, superficial societies of Vienna, Prague, and Salzburg deigned to idolize him—he was just as often alone and poor and searching.

At the end, desperately sick and burdened with pain, he managed to go on working on his *Requiem*. He never finished it.

The clocks had just struck midnight in Vienna on December 5, 1791, when the black skies loosed a torrent of rain. The continuing storm prevented practically everyone from going to the cemetery. The undistinguished body of a once pretty child whose genius had sung for far-too-few years was tossed into a pauper's grave. He was only thirty-five.

CHAPTER SIX

Import and Export – and Beethoven

Luigi Cherubini (1760–1842) was one of France's "imported" composers who—like Lully, Meyerbeer, Gluck, and Offenbach—played a major part in her musical history. One can suppose that Cherubini, as a young student in Italy—when he was busy copying thousands of pages of other musicians' works and acting as a "ghost writer" for his teacher—might have had dreams of grandeur and delusions about one day becoming the commander in chief of French music. That is conjecture, but the copying certainly gave him a knowledge of the architecture of music—which he mastered and never lost control of—and his "ghosting" enabled him to hear his student endeavors performed by the finest artists of the day. Let us clarify that it was once common practice for teachers to let their pupils compose arias and recitatives for inclusion in the master's operas.

At twenty, when his work made its official, so to speak, debut, Cherubini was hardly acclaimed as a major talent. The reaction was so unspectacular that he welcomed an invitation to come to London. There, Italian opera was still amusing the public. Cherubini managed to amuse the Prince of Wales and get himself appointed the composer to the King, but his opera, *Giulio Sabino* (1786) was a flop.

Never one to stay in enemy territory unless it afforded tremendous possibilities, Cherubini took the next Channel boat, and before the year was out he found himself rather well set up in the fabulous court of Marie Antoinette.

Although he was successful at graciously working himself into the social life of Paris, musical acclaim did not come overnight. As a matter of fact, it was not until he returned from a stay in Turin, Italy, where he saw his *Iphigenia in Aulide* produced, that things started looking up operatically. *Démophon,* his first French opera, was not a great success, but it impressed some of the critics who were intelligent enough to hear the glimmer of something new.

It appears that hairdressers then were a musical bunch of fellows. One was, at least—Marie Antoinette's. She gave him permission to open an opera company, and he chose Cherubini as its director.

His next opera, *Ladoïska,* with its unusual harmonies and new instrumental effects, took the Parisians by storm. However, as other works followed, the warm sounds of applause and the silver sounds of royal compliments made way for the rumbles of Revolution, and Cherubini hastened to Normandy. The Imperial Theater in Vienna invited him to write an opera in 1805. It was produced there, but the war between Austria and France rather upset his plans for making any grand headway in Vienna. He went back to France and sullenly "retired."

Friends cunningly convinced Cherubini that he had to write some music for the consecration of the church near his villa. The success of his *Mass in F* was something of an inspiration, and he decided to concentrate more on sacred music, which he remembered he had had an affinity for when he was sixteen. The glory that he had dreamed of engulfed him almost immediately. Napoleon, who had never really admired Cherubini, now honored him. He was voted into the Institute, was appointed the head of the King's Chapel, and then became the Director of the Conservatory.

There, in the all-powerful command of one of the world's leading music schools, he could dictate his doctrines and wield the musical force he had long wanted. It was his position, not his operas—as he had imagined—that brought him absolute rule over French music and anyone connected with it. It is interesting that this Italian-alien commandant closed the Conservatory's doors to everyone who was not French. Director Cherubini even classified Liszt and Mendelssohn as foreigners when they requested entrance to his hallowed domain! As a composer of both religious and operatic works, Cherubini was convinced that the idea was the motivation of all good music. For some, though, despite their breadth and unity, his works are pervaded by a dry seriousness and a tense calm. Even his masterpiece, *Médeé* (*Medea*) for all its drama, seems held back by the composer's own self-imposed, immovable walls of taste and integrity. Although it is easy to imagine that his excess of taste did not make him enduringly popular with excited Revolutionary audiences, we must admit that he—as a composer and a musical dictator—was a force that exerted itself on many composers and styles. Beethoven was one who was definitely aware of his work.

The popularity of Cherubini's vengeful *Medea* eventually waned. She was relegated to library shelves until Maria Callas

—in 1953—proved that great singing, great acting, and a real understanding of Cherubini's style could bring the composer and his heroine to life in a manner that was impressive to atomic-age operagoers.

Cherubini was not Napoleon's favorite composer. A son of Italian peasants, Gasparo Spontini (1774–1851), honestly and openly claimed that honor.

As a child, Spontini's musical ambitions were constantly thwarted by a determined uncle who tried to force him into the priesthood. The boy finally got up the courage to run away. Later, while he was a student at the Naples conservatory, his narrow-minded professors refused to let him accept a commission from the famous Teatro Argentina in Rome, so he ran away again. His Roman success made Paris the next obvious steppingstone to operatic fame. But once he was there, Spontini realized that he, too, would have to bow before the French nationalistic jealousies and whims if he had any serious intentions of making his name in the music capital.

He failed to please, let alone impress, the blasé French until his opera *Milton* (1804) gained him something of a foothold and a little affection from the Parisian elite. In addition, the press accused *Milton* of being decidedly un-Neapolitan—indeed, they said, poor Spontini could not have written it! Spontini's fortune changed when he was offered the libretto to *La Vestale* (*The Vestal Virgin*)—a piece that Cherubini had never gotten around to doing. *The Vestal Virgin* was a resounding success when it was first performed in 1807, and within the next dozen years it chalked up more than two hundred performances.

His next opera, *Fernand Cortez,* was vigorously admired by

Napoleon. He probably cared little for its musical worth, but since he was planning a war against Spain, he was convinced that its Spanish theme would do much to turn the tide of public opinion in his direction. *Cortez* was not another *Vestale*.

Spontini bided his time by becoming the chief conductor of the celebrated Comédie Française when it was united with the Italian Opera.

His last opera, *Agnes von Hohenstaufen* (1827), was written during the years that he conducted for the Berlin Opera. It shows, as all of his works for the theater do, that he and opera were at the end of a long line—the line that had clung tenaciously to Gluck's dramatic ideas. Spontini, like Gluck, had an intellectual temperament that held firm check on the use of effect for effect's sake.

We must not regard classic operatic music as being merely dull, for it was more than that. To listeners today it is occasionally trying, but it is also important because it led to the romantic movement.

During the classical period one had to abide by stringent laws and traditional forms. These gave way as the people loosened themselves from the pressures of the nobility. With this freedom came a new kind of spontaneity for music and the theater. Blood and revolution caused man not only to reconsider the absolute necessity of personal dignity and individuality—he also began to think of his fellow man. Classic stories of gods and their godlike problems, accompanied by formal music, were toppled from their marble pedestals in favor of more personal ideas. Also, the fever pitch of the times carried a stronger, and much more likely to be displayed, set of emotional values. The middle class pushed on, and all the arts found themselves facing a new audience.

During the Empire period, opera, with its love of grand spectacle, was predominantly occupied with singing about the immortal causes of the Revolution, the needs of the country, and the government of the people. And it is well to remember that, although French opera was never produced in Italy, it was performed in Germany. Consequently, it was to be expected that French opera and its romantic tendencies would influence German composers. One was Beethoven.

Ludwig van Beethoven (1770–1827) was of the classic period, but his stormy personality could not be held within those confining barriers. There were kindlier souls, perhaps, who quietly refused to recognize that a restraining force existed, but it took Beethoven to demand *why* it did.

Unlike the composers who had preceded him, including the clever showmen and the slick craftsmen, he could not make use of—much less accept—timeworn traditions.

As a composer he was destined to write some of the greatest music the world has ever known, and his music shaped his personal destiny, too. He was born into a time that also claimed the genius of Wordsworth and Napoleon. He inherited his musicianship from generations of Beethovens before him. He also inherited complex, desperate frustrations that were to hover around him like some angel of darkness—these from a grandmother and father who looked for an escape from their troubled lives by drinking themselves to death.

His childhood was incredibly miserable and made endurable only by his beautiful mother. Johann, his father, was an insen-

sitive boor who drunkenly dreamed of making his son a duplication of the boy wonder, Mozart.

Gifted he was, but Ludwig hardly fitted into such a category. Poor teachers and poorer teaching methods did more to
repress his talents than develop them. Fortunately, at the age of
ten, he began to study with Christian Neefe. It took Neefe, a
court organist and a natural teacher, no time at all to recognize
the young boy's unusual musical abilities and, more important,
his proud and questioning mind. At thirteen, Ludwig was
made an assistant court organist, and three years later he was
exposed to the cultural and musical life of Vienna where he
met Mozart.

His beloved mother died that year, and this deprivation set
off a series of psychological reactions that were to plague him
for the rest of his life. At nineteen, in order to protect his
brothers from their drunken, irresponsible father, he arranged
to be made the head of the family.

With this new burden on his mind, he went again to
Vienna.

Although symphonies, concertos, and sonatas that were to
make him immortal occupied his years there, there was always
the thought in the back of his mind that he had to write an
opera. That the opera composers in Vienna were certainly
more handsomely compensated for their efforts than ordinary
composers might have had some influence on this desire.

When we consider that Beethoven found Da Ponte's libretto
for *Don Giovanni* questionable morally, we realize that he certainly set himself a difficult task of finding a libretto that
would fulfill his own demands—demands that music must glo-
rify man's freedom and the eternal need for justice.

He found it in a play by Jean Nicolas Bouilly, *Léonore,* an absurd melodrama that was a smash hit in Paris. Beethoven was immediately smitten with its characters—villainous Pizzaro, the virtuous Léonore, who saves her political-prisoner husband, Florestan, by disguising herself as a boy—and remained oblivious to all of its bad writing and its thick dullness during all the time he composed and reworked his operatic version.

Leonore opened in 1805. The November, Viennese atmosphere was tense and gloomy, and the streets were filled with Napoleon's army of occupation. *Leonore* was a dismal failure.

Beethoven shortened its three acts to two, rewrote some of the text, and gave it a new overture. In this new version it was a modest success, but then the composer had an argument with the head of the Hoftheater and refused to let it be performed again.

Nine years later Beethoven decided to rework it again. Treitschke, an excellent writer, also sliced away at the libretto with his literary scalpel, and at its next presentation, in 1814, *Fidelio,* as it was now called, was a sensation.

With all this reworking there are four *Leonore* overtures, and they still create problems and arguments. Audiences who have never heard a note of the opera have become well acquainted with the heroine because all the overtures are among the standard repertoire of all symphony orchestras.

It is possible that *Leonore No. 1* was the first, but some believe it was planned for a performance in 1807 that didn't materialize. *Leonore No. 2* was composed for the premiere of 1805 that resulted in a failure. *No. 3* appeared at the 1806 performances. Superb dramatic music that it is, it did not enhance the opera. The 1814 performances were preceded by *another* overture—the one we know today as the *Fidelio*.

Gustav Mahler, the Viennese composer-conductor, started the practice of playing the *Leonore No. 3* between the two scenes of the second act.

There is no doubt that Beethoven was a magnificent dramatic composer; this does not imply that his magnificence encompassed being able to write dramatic music for the theater. The stage, its technicalities, and especially its singing actors were something his imagination could not comprehend. He also felt constricted by having to relegate his orchestra to second place because of the demands of the drama and the vocal lines. Leonore's thrilling *scena* and aria, *"Abscheulicher, wo eilst du hin?"* ("Infamous tyrant! Where are you going in such haste?"), contains more genuine drama and emotion than interminable minutes of the oftentimes dull score. It is a challenge and ambition of all great dramatic sopranos.

Fidelio was the Vienna debut role of Wilhelmine Schröder (later Schröder-Devrient) in 1822. She was barely eighteen at the time, and her breath-takingly dramatic conception of the taxing role was responsible for the opera's reaching a pinnacle of success that it had never known.

Wilhelmine had been an actress and dancer before turning to operatic singing. Her emotional performances—with little attention paid to the necessities of *bel canto*—soon established her as a major star. They also brought her to the attention of Wagner. Through Schröder-Devrient a new species came to life—the German dramatic soprano.

Fidelio with its trumpet calls of freedom, its soaring declarations of love, and its shafts of musical sunlight was chosen to open the new Vienna State Opera after the Second World War. Tragically, the theater had been destroyed by American bombs, but the opera-loving Viennese, poor and rich alike, contributed their own money and efforts, and the Vienna State Opera was reconstructed in exact and loving duplication of its original glory.

Beethoven was obsessed by demons and by ideas—ideas of freedom, heroism, and the true capacity of man's soul. The demons that pursued him and the ideas that liberated him live and breathe—and sometimes erupt—in his music. If he was unable to make *Fidelio* a completely great opera, he was able to make it, as Victor Gollancz says: ". . . hymn to the unconditional sacredness of individual personality—of every 'single, separate' human being." In freeing himself he liberated music from the restrictions of the classic form and carried it to mountaintops where it sang out against the elements of time and urged the world to listen to the needs of man.

CHAPTER SEVEN

Carl Maria von Weber and Romantic Opera

To many, Carl Maria von Weber means the *Invitation to the Dance,* a sentimental perfumed piece of music whose only possible claim to immortality is the fact that it eventually became a ballet with a closing scene that included a spectacular leap through an open, stage window . . . a leap by a rose-petaled god of the dance, the Russian Waslaw Nijinsky. But that is unfair to Weber, for he was *the* important influence on all romantic opera. Rarely now, even in Germany, do his operas see the light of day. Once in a while, a diva will dare the sometimes inconsiderate bravura of his arias. More than occasionally, his overtures to *Der Freischütz, Oberon,* and *Euryanthe* are listed on symphonic programs. But Weber is no longer the rage.

In investigating the composer's life we are faced again with the father-son, hoped-for prodigy syndrome. Mozart changed the world of music, for which we are grateful, but the Wolfgang-Leopold success story must also have caused a lot of unhappy tantrums for other musical families. The Weber family was one.

Carl Maria (1786–1826) was the son of Franz Anton von

Weber, a gentleman of somewhat questionable talents and un-reasonable ambitions. The elder Weber was known to play at politics and meddle in music. His son had barely stopped crawl-ing, let alone begun to enjoy a normal childhood, when papa set out with him on a grand tour. Franz wanted to show the world that Carl Maria was another Mozart. He wasn't.

The years spent with his father's group of traveling "actors" took their toll on the boy's frail physique. But, for a future composer, they were not wasted years. He learned many things about the techniques and the "show business" methods of thea-ter that would prove valuable to him.

His first serious music studies were with Abbé Vogler in Vi-enna. Vogler was neither a first-class musician nor a remarkable teacher, but he could offer a commodity that was as necessary in Weber's day as it is now—influential connections. Vogler was completely captivated by Carl Maria's obvious musical-ity, his aggressive personality and his charm. The young com-poser had not celebrated his eighteenth birthday before he was offered the position of conductor for the Breslau Opera. There is slight doubt that the boy was surely recommended by Vog-ler.

More important though, is the fact that Carl Maria hap-pened to be a first-rate conductor. The bourgeois townspeople of Breslau, as well as the directors of the Opera, might have ad-vanced themselves if they had cooperated with his demands for serious musical discipline. Demands generally only antagonize, as we know, and Weber's did exactly that. Consumed by bore-dom and disappointment, Weber quit his post to join the musi-cal court of the Duke of Württemberg.

Later, when the war against Napoleon required that the

Duke spend some time at the battlefront, his patron set Carl
Maria up in the ungrateful job of being secretary to his
brother, Ludwig. The unlikely job didn't propel young Weber's musical career, but it did introduce him to a life that he
found delightfully compatible. The atmosphere of carefree
companions, a lot of wine, and a romantic soprano, Margar-
ethe Lang.

The *dolce vita* also introduced him to a complicated situation that resulted in banishment for both him and his father.

To make a living he returned to the concert stage, as a pian-
ist, and he eventually settled in Darmstadt. There he met
Jakob Liebmann Beer. Beer was also an Abbé Vogler protégé.
The two composers became fast friends, and the seventeen-
year-old Beer's already zooming career seems to have inspired
Carl Maria to concentrate on some real work.

Darmstadt was only the beginning of Beer's fame. He was
getting ready to change his untheatrical name to Meyerbeer
and excite the operatic world.

Carl Maria rewrote his first opera, *Das Stumme
Waldmädchen* (*The Dumb Girl of the Forest*) and retitled it
Silvana. It was produced in Frankfurt, 1810. Ironically, the pre-
miere's competition of the evening was a glamorous Madame
Blanchard, whose present *succès fou* was to amuse the popu-
lace by going "up, up, and away" in a balloon.

Due to the spectacular La Blanchard, the *Silvana* audience
was practically nonexistent, and Weber was ignored until the
following year when he completed his *singspiel, Abu Hassan*.
Successful as that was, Weber did not write another work for
the stage until 1817. After his father's death, Weber accepted
the position of Director of the Opera in Prague. The Czech

theater needed him badly, and for the three years that he was in Prague Weber reorganized the company and made it a major opera house.

The year 1817 was the real beginning for Weber. He married soprano Caroline Brandt and began work on *Der Freischütz* (*The Freeshooter*). The weird, legendary story of the Devil—in the guise of the Black Huntsman—and seven silver bullets had fascinated Weber for a long time. He had great affection for the musical climate and tastes of Berlin, so he promised the premiere to the opera house there. Little did he realize that its first performance would be postponed, then postponed again, and still more regrettable, it would finally be judged by a city which was devoted to Spontini!

It took one performance of *Der Freischütz*—on a June night in 1821—and the fickle Berlin public to prove that Spontini was on the way out and von Weber was the new king of opera.

Berlin shouted its approval, and critics and cities all over Germany fought for future productions. His opera sang about things close to the hearts of all Germans. *Der Freischütz* was unashamedly theatrical, it was rife with mystery, and it exalted the romantic purity of its gentle heroine.

Weber, with *Der Freischütz,* was the first composer to throw caution to the winds and abandon everything classic. True, the time was ripe for German romantic opera. But that was not the only reason for its amazing success. He had given the people, for the first time, music they could identify with. His music breathed the winds of the Black Forest and praised the simplicity of their lives. Audiences were quick to hear that *their* Weber's music was free of Italian trickery, and *their* singers were singing in German. Also Weber was very skillful in his writing for the orchestra and he knew, from childhood experience in dozens of theaters, exactly when and where his operas needed applause-getters—necessary gimmicks that are still sought after by producers and composers of our present-day musical comedies.

His opera had a spectacular success in London (1824) with the English title *The Seventh Bullet,* and Americans took it to their hearts in 1825. Inspired by one triumph after another, Weber decided to take another step forward—he would go beyond the success of his folklore opera and create a romantic work with all the grandeur of the greatest court operas. This time he dispensed with all spoken dialogue (which he had used in *Der Freischütz*) and made the sad mistake of selecting a libretto that to this day has probably not been equaled for its utter insanity. The mixed-up story has something to do with romantic French history. Neither it nor Weber's music was received with much approval at its Vienna premiere (1823). *Euryanthe,* the title of the ill-fated piece, contains some lovely music. It was—and is—rarely performed.

Charles Kemble, director of the Covent Garden Opera, London, commissioned Weber to write an opera for his theater and *Oberon* (or *The Elf King's Oath*) is the result. It had its first performance in 1826, and the English audiences liked it well enough to demand its repetition some thirty times that season. In *Oberon,* Weber returned to the use of spoken dialogue, and this time his libretto stumbled around through three different worlds—the court of Charlemagne, a mysterious fairyland, and exotic Baghdad! There are remarkable musical moments in *Oberon,* especially in the big soprano aria, *"Ozean, du Ungeheuer!"* ("Ocean, Thou Mighty Monster!") and overture.

Weber's instrumental innovations in *Oberon* and his use of a richly textured orchestra were clearly inspirations for Wagner and Debussy.

The tubercular composer was dead before he was forty. At his burial in Dresden, the music of *Euryanthe* was played at his tomb, and Richard Wagner, who was destined to carry romantic German opera into realms that Weber had not dreamed possible, gave voice to an emotional and moving funeral oration.

Romantic opera and its love of the supernatural also tempted other composers, but none can be said to have completely and successfully measured up to or surpassed Weber.

Heinrich Marschner (1795–1861) first attracted attention with his opera *Der Vampyr* (*The Vampire*). Wagner improved on that ghoulish story with his own *Der fliegende Holländer* (*The Flying Dutchman*). Marschner also did a version of *Ivanhoe* which he called *Der Templer und die Jüdin*.

Another popular *singspiel* of the early eighteenth century was Kreutzer's *Das Nachtlager in Granada* (*The Night-Camp at Granada*).

Gustav Albert Lortzing's *Zar und Zimmerman* (*Czar and Carpenter*) was premiered with resounding success in 1837 and is still performed in German opera houses.

Otto Nicolai's *Die lustigen Weiber von Windsor* (*The Merry Wives of Windsor*) was first heard in Berlin in 1849, and its delightful combination of both German and Italian music styles still enchants opera audiences—so much, in fact, that it has also been made into a colorful film.

Friedrich von Flotow's name is kept before the public with occasional revivals of his *Martha*. The Metropolitan Opera in

New York saw fit to do this less than brilliant work in a sumptuous production during the 1967–1968 season. Its bittersweet
and sentimental aria for soprano, "The Last Rose of Summer,"
seems destined to be remembered whether its heroine is or not.

Karl Millöcker's *Der Bettelstudent* (*The Beggar Student*)
also retains its popularity in Europe, and his light operas, such
as *"Die Dubarry,"* still attract audiences—if the leading lady is
a glamorous and popular personality.

The seed of romantic opera that was presented in Beethoven's *Fidelio* was set into the German soil by Carl Maria von
Weber. With *Der Freischütz* he proved that romantic love,
love of nature and love of self could be expressed in musical
terms that had not been suspected by classic, objective minds.
His subjective legends, his woods and witches and kings—enhanced by orchestral and vocal settings of perfect collaboration
—were the vibrant roadways that led poets, songwriters, and
Wagner to the moon-struck cliffs and pounding shores of ro-
manticism.

CHAPTER EIGHT

Meyerbeer and Berlioz

There was never any doubt that Carl Maria von Weber's friend, Jakob Liebmann Beer, would not achieve all his ambitions. He had the good fortune to be the offspring of a family of bankers. A background of culture and cash afforded him every chance to cultivate his clever imagination and his consuming desire to be famous.

German-born, he was a sought-after virtuoso pianist when he was only nine.

That he differed from Weber was clearly defined at their first meeting. Weber was the perfect nationalistic German. Beer was a young internationalist. Always well off, he inherited even more money from a relative on the promise that he would change his name. Jakob, with his eyes on fame and success and with Italy as his first goal, complied with the request and changed not only his last name but his first. He became known as Giacomo Meyerbeer.

He absorbed what he needed from Rossini, experienced considerable success with several of his own operas, and turned his back on Weber's suggestions that he write a true German opera.

His *Il Crociato in Egitto* (*The Crusade in Egypt*) created a bit of excitement at its first performance in Venice (1824). Two years later he was in Paris proudly taking part in its first French presentation. From then until 1831 he produced no new operas, but he was far from idle. He had fallen in love with Paris, with French history, and with the French language. No aspect of anything French went unnoticed. He virtually lived in French libraries and museums and studied the complex French personality. His studies paid off and eventually his new-found "rapport," his craftsmanship, and his showmanship reached the stage where history openly credited him with the destiny of French grand opera. Two native Frenchmen, Louis Veron, a producer-director, and Eugène Scribe, a librettist, were the other members of the triumvirate that was the backbone of authentic French opera.

Meyerbeer, who had an extraordinary ego force and would do anything to be popular, knew that complete "success" meant giving his audience what it wanted. Parisians demanded spectacle and Meyerbeer was not one to disappoint them. Simplicity and simple folk bored him. He flooded the stage of L'Opera de Paris with grandiose, historical works that were musically and scenically far beyond anything that Cherubini or Spontini had afforded French operagoers.

Meyerbeer, Veron, and Scribe were completely agreeable and adaptable to the several rules one had to obey for guaranteed success—rules that exist today, rightly or wrongly, in all the entertainment fields, including opera. Impresarios and composers and singers continue to remember that audiences want what they want. If the item sells—sell it again.

During Meyerbeer's time audiences wanted great dramatic

pageants. Massive choruses, ballets, and violently historical plots suddenly pushed aside Mozart's ideas of what opera should be.

Meyerbeer put everything he had into *Robert le Diable* (*Robert the Devil*). Scribe supplied him with a script offering him innumerable opportunities for melody, dramatic orchestral effects, and a bit of the supernatural. The romantic and fantastic legend became a triumph for both him and Meyerbeer. The opera's first night, in 1831, was an occasion for hysterical enthusiasm.

Les Huguenots, his second French opera, was a musical drama about ill-fated lovers and stormy sixteenth-century times when France and her society were torn apart by religious wars. It was heard in 1836. *Les Huguenots* blasted its audiences with blaring military bands and thundering choruses. Its leading roles were created especially for "stars"—seven stars, in fact. It is understandable that opera houses today find it difficult to cast such a work.

Consider that the cast list at early Metropolitan opera performances included all these Golden Age stars: Lillian Nordica, the soprano from Maine, Australia's Nellie Melba, Victor Maurel, and the de Reszke brothers from France, and the Italian mezzo Sofia Scalchi. La Scala in Milan has braved *Les Huguenots* in recent years but only when it could boast of artists like Joan Sutherland, another Australian, and Italy's dramatic Giullieta Simionato.

In 1842 Meyerbeer was invited by the King of Prussia to become the Music Director of the Berlin opera. While there he got around to writing a German opera, *Das Feldlager in Schlesien* (*An Army Camp in Silesia*), whose performances were illuminated by the appearances of the now-legendary Jenny Lind.

Jenny Lind was—with Henriette Sontag and Adelina Patti —at the top of the list of extraordinary coloratura sopranos during the 1800s. These sopranos had voices that were particularly suited to singing the agile, fluid style of vocal music so popular at the time.

It is important that we establish a line of definition regarding these virtuoso sopranos and what is accepted in many quarters today as a coloratura.

During the time of Meyerbeer, Rossini, and Bellini it was understood that every soprano could and did sing dramatically, lyrically, and had a command of coloratura. Not so today, when the specialized coloratura that graces the stages of leading opera houses and the Ed Sullivan show cannot begin to duplicate the historically documented ability to sing in all soprano categories. There are exceptions, of course, and they will be introduced later on.

Jenny Lind was one of the thoroughly schooled singers of the period, whose shimmering, pure quality of voice and sweetness of sound particularly enhanced the coloratura ornamentation that intrigued the public of that time. She was born in Sweden, in 1820. She made her debut at fifteen and soon became the leading opera star of Stockholm. Miss Lind, personally, was something of an enigma. She was uncommonly plain in appearance, a religious fanatic, full of false morality, yet dedicated to the colorful life of a "star." Her moral reasons kept her from ever singing in France or Italy, but they allowed her to tour the United States under the guidance of the less than artistic P. T. Barnum, of circus fame.

Berliners adored her, and eventually Meyerbeer conducted only at her performances in that city.

The English quickly succumbed to her—her stage personality, that is—and her voice. She was the exact opposite of temperamental prima donnas they had been exposed to and they welcomed her radiant and seemingly natural feminine simplicity and her ability to create an aura of everything that was good.

The clever press agentry of Barnum helped to create a fortune for her in the United States. Without him she did less well, and as her public came to realize that she was far from the lovely angel who was capable of singing everything (including "The Last Rose of Summer"), its rhapsodic admiration began to diminish.

No matter—she was a genuine coloratura singer and she was a product of the age of grand opera.

In 1847, while Jenny Lind was the idol of all London, Meyerbeer was producing *Rienzi,* Wagner's early opera. Richard Wagner would later become Meyerbeer's hated rival.

Thirteen years after *Les Huguenots,* Meyerbeer was back in Paris with a new opera, *Le Prophète,* (1849).

Le Prophète was another authentic, French grand opera, and it is interesting to note that it had its American premiere in New Orleans in 1850. New Orleans was the first city in the United States to welcome opera and present it in spectacular style. The French general and statesman Lafayette, who joined Washington's army in 1777, was one of many European celebrities who have been quoted as calling the Théâtre d'Orléans equal in décor and performance to any of the great theaters in Europe.

Meyerbeer's *Les Huguenots* was a favorite of New Orleans. And as Ronald L. Davis points out in his admirable book, *A History of Opera in the American West,* careful research has proved that many operas were premiered in New Orleans that New York and Philadelphia have taken the credit for. Giacomo Meyerbeer's last opera, *L'Africaine* (*The African Maid*), was not given until almost a year after his death in 1864.

As a composer, manager (the Paris Opéra and Berlin), shrewd showman, and innovator, Meyerbeer was a talent to be reckoned with. He knew the orchestra and the human voice. And above all he knew the heady impact of drama. He knew how to create thrilling climaxes and how to grip and hold his audiences with every theatrical trick. Even Wagner, who hated Meyerbeer, used all of his colleague's knowledge to increase the potential of his own dramatic ideas.

At this time things were also happening in the lighter field of operetta and *opéra comique.*

Operetta has often suffered at the hands of her critics because her main objective is to please and to amuse. But there is nothing so terribly wrong with tunes that are catchy and can be whistled; we find them in Verdi and Puccini in abundance. Be that as it may, operetta with its spoken dialogue and satirical ambitions is looked down upon by some. So is the French *opéra comique* which is burdened with a split personality. It has its lighthearted and gay librettos, and its spoken dialogue might also be amusing. But there are also works in this style that are distinctly not comedies. Actually they are extremely serious.

Adolphe-Charles Adam (1803–1856) wrote an operetta in 1836, *Le Postillon de Longjumeau* (*The Postman of Longju-*

meau), that entertains audiences today. Particularly when the leading tenor is able to pour out a series of high C's and D's to delight his admirers.

Probably the most prolific composer of this brilliant type of amusement was Jacques Offenbach (1819–1880). Offenbach was born in Germany. Strangely enough, as if to prove that Germans got around, he strikes everyone as being more French than champagne or the Seine. He was the mod-fashion plate of his day, and between frequent appearances at all the "in" places of Paris he managed to write about ninety operas and operettas. His *Les Contes d'Hoffmann* (*The Tales of Hoffmann*) still holds its place in the repertory of many opera houses. *Hoffmann*'s fantasy plot calls for three star sopranos. In recent times these roles have become something of a challenging tour de force for prima donnas. One, Beverly Sills, a fine American singer, has successfully negotiated the pitfalls of all three roles in the same performance!

Other Offenbach operettas that are performed today include *Orphée aux enfers* (*Orpheus in the Underworld*), *La belle Hélène* (*The Beautiful Helen*), and *La vie parisienne* (*Parisian Life*). To the more easily amused audiences of our time they continue to epitomize all the glamour of the can-can and that "real" Paris of our imaginations.

The superficial charm of operetta held no interest for Hector Berlioz (1803–1869). Music, thoughts about freeing music, and the desire to be a musician dominated him from early boyhood. Unfortunately, his doctor-father was not so artistically inclined, and Hector obediently had to make an attempt to follow in his medical footsteps. Disgusted as Hector was with the horrors of the college dissecting arena and its bloody cadavers,

he did his best to stay on at school. He found that he couldn't.
Not long after he began his studies at the austere Conservatory
of Music he realized he was also not in tune with that famous
school's outdated methods of teaching. In addition, his father
angrily cut him off from any monetary assistance, and the following years found him in a state of poverty. With no one to
believe in his new musical ideas and no seeming changes in a
string of negative reactions to his recently composed orchestral
works, he tried to drown himself. Fortunately, two established
composers, Schumann and Chopin, caught him before the
waves did. Surely a gift of gratitude is due these two musicians
—over and above their other contributions.

Success and any apparent understanding of his music was a
long time in coming. Meyerbeer and Offenbach held all of
Paris' chichi music world in the palms of their hands, and another composer—Wagner—was doing his best to break down
any available doors. The idea that he had a mission in music
occupied Berlioz' mind and his creations for almost a quarter of
a century. He believed that he was meant to revolutionize opera—beyond what Gluck had done. Berlioz wanted to liberate
the music of France from the outside traditions with which
composers like Offenbach and Meyerbeer were stifling it. He
wrote: "I want music to be proudly free, to be victorious. Liberty is a necessity. Liberty of heart, of mind, of soul—of everything." Part of Berlioz' uniqueness was this sense of liberty,
and that his very personal music touched the imagination and
soul of the new masses—the young people who were tasting de-
mocracy for the first time.

Berlioz was not primarily an operatic composer. His preference lay with the Germanic—the symphonic idea of the orches-

tra as drama—rather than with the Italian idea that opera was song and it was for singers. His strictly orchestral works are played constantly, but his four stage works—*Lélio; ou la Retour à la vie* (*Lélio; or the Return to Life*) (1830), *Benvenuto Cellini* (1838), *Les Troyens* (1863), and *Béatrice et Bénédict* (1862), are rarely performed today. That is, unless an enterprising conductor, like Thomas Scherman with his Little Orchestra Society in New York City (this group has introduced many of Berlioz' works to American audiences), decides that it is time again for their beauties to be disclosed to modern ears.

Lélio is not really an operatic work, so *Benvenuto Cellini* gets the honor of being his first opera premiere. It was hardly a success. The six acts of *Les Troyens* tell the story of the fall of Troy and the legendary events that followed. Berlioz adapted his libretto from sections of Vergil's *Aeneid* and called the first part (two acts) *La Prise de Troie* (*The Capture of Troy*). The second part is known as *Les Troyens à Carthage* (*The Trojans at Carthage*).

The staging demands and the necessity of casting the numerous important roles with major singers make the opera impractical to produce. Also, neither American nor European operagoers seem able to make up their minds as to whether *Les Troyens* is the greatest opera of the nineteenth century or the most colossal bore of several centuries.

Berlioz authorities like Scherman, Jacques Barzun, and Donald Jay Grout are of the opinion that the work is deserving of repeated hearings until musicians, performers, *and* the public are made to understand its unique dramatic and musical qualities.

Three operas—or three hundred—is of little interest when

considering the fantastic Berlioz contributions to music. His
Requiem with its orchestra of nearly two hundred instruments
(sixteen kettledrums), extra brass choirs, and two hundred
singers may have shocked and startled the first listeners, but it
and all his works expanded the orchestra and gave it new life
and color. He knew the value of light and dark, soft and loud,
and his combinations of instruments were unheard of for his
time.

His brilliant book on orchestration has probably been de-
voured by more hopeful and successful composers and conductors than any volume of its kind.

He was different—not just to *be* different—but because his
romantic ideas demanded that he live with himself, with his
music, and with his ambitions, no matter what his popular acclaim.

His music sang from his heart. And the people listened.

CHAPTER NINE

Rossini, Donizetti, and Some More Singers

The study of Rossini and his operas brings pleasure and relief. He was a successful composer and he lived his life successfully. For the most part the jealousy, hatred, and intrigue that burdened (and perhaps inspired) many other composers, did not influence him. He derived genuine pleasure from helping others. He cared for his family with warmth and affection—as well as financially. Four countries made no bones about their love and admiration for him, and he entertained with wit and style. In other words, he lived as well as he wrote music.

Gioacchino Rossini (1792–1868) was born in Italy—an Italy where every town, village, and city boasted at least a modest opera house. His mother was a singer, his father a professional trumpet player, and their constant traveling around the country made it necessary for them to leave Gioacchino Antonio with relatives. He grew up practically on his own with a negligible education and a strong desire to be a musician.

At eighteen he had his first taste of success; his one-act opera *La Cambiale di Matrimonio* (*The Marriage Contract*) was performed in Venice. The applause ringing in his ears and the lira lining his pockets convinced him that being an opera composer was his rightful predestination.

During his twentieth year he saw five of his operas produced, and three years later his list of stage works had increased to fourteen! Admittedly all these were not unqualified successes. But Rossini was not only young and handsome, he was blessed with a sense of honesty about himself. He accepted his failures and went right on composing.

One of his great Venetian successes was *L'Italiana in Algerì* (*The Italian girl in Algiers*). Later in life he often recalled his affection for the people of Venice because they had suffered through his bad operas as well as his good ones.

Naples capitulated to the young Rossini when his *Elisabetta, Regina d'Inghilterra* (*Elizabeth, Queen of England*) was premiered in 1815. The origin of this opera is as amusing as many of the composer's operas. Rossini had the good fortune to be invited by Domenico Barbaia, the director of several major opera houses, to join the staff of his opera house in Naples. The San Carlo was one of the great opera houses in Italy, and Barbaia's lady friend, Isabella Colbran, was the power behind the power. She was also one of the San Carlo's leading singers, and Rossini, never one to waste much time in writing an opera *or* conquering a lovely lady, calculatedly wrote *Elizabeth* for her. No doubt her stunning appearance and her dramatic ability played a part in the opera's success. In addition to her obvious talents, her devotion to Rossini was expressed in a musical way that was at that time unheard of. She permitted him to strike out any and all coloratura ornamentation in every one of her arias. One can imagine that there were many raised eyebrows and much conversation among other singers—singers at that time took it as a matter of fact that they could ornament anything they wished to!

Rome was not as easily convinced as Venice and Naples had been that Rossini was a great opera composer. His newest work, *Il Barbiere di Siviglia* (*The Barber of Seville*) (1816), was performed before an audience that was predominantly made up of a claque hired by the veteran composer, Giovanni Paisiello. They saw to it that *Barber* was a disaster. Its second performance—without the disapproving claque—held its own, and Rome admitted to some of its charm. Within several years, the *Barber* and Rossini were the talk of every country in Europe. By 1825, Americans were applauding it and its famous tenor, Manuel García (1775–1832).

García was a Spanish gypsy and one of the greatest tenors of his day. He was a great favorite of Rossini's, and the composer had written the role of Almaviva with García in mind. Almaviva's aria, *"Ecco ridente"* ("Lo, in the lovely sky the golden dawn is breaking"), is a perfect example of Rossini's style and the ornamentations used by singers and composers of the nineteenth century.

The García family was important to the whole Rossini era. Manuel García's two daughters, Maria Malibran and Pauline Viardot-García became operatic singers of legend. His son, Manuel (Patricio Rodriguez) García, became the most famous voice teacher of the nineteenth century.

Maria Malibran (1808–1836) started studying singing with her famous father at fifteen. The quality of her voice labeled her a contralto, but her range and extraordinary technical command allowed her to sing virtuoso soprano roles as well. Her first appearance, in London, as Rosina in *The Barber of Seville*, was a sensation. Her tempestuous personality and acting ability struck immediate fire with audiences, and it was not long before she was the rage of Paris. She did nothing in moderation, and it is said that her stage performances took so much out of her, vocally and physically, that she had to stop singing from time to time in order to recover. Her extravagant personality was greeted with triumphs in America and all over Europe. She was a "star" to the very end. In 1836 she was thrown from a horse, and for the months that followed, she was in great pain. Nine days before she died she made her last triumphant appearance. One of the great singers of all time was dead at twenty-eight!

Her sister, Pauline, was not the flamboyant, "theatrical" singer that Maria was. Nor were the Rossini roles exactly right for her. She established herself as a major singer in the operas of Meyerbeer. The two of them are also responsible for what we now think of as the mezzo-soprano "star." Pauline Viardot met Meyerbeer in Berlin and he kept his promise to her that she would sing the role of Fides in his *Le Prophète* at its first Paris performance. Although, as an artist and intellect, she was vastly finer than her sister, she also shared Maria's determination and ambition to sing everything. The pressures and the strain eventually took their toll, and she retired from the stage when she was barely past forty. She became one of the great teachers of singing and died at the age of eighty-nine.

The Barber of Seville takes its place with *Le Nozze di Figaro* as a perfect example of great *opera buffa*. From the first note of its overture to its joyous ending it is rich with timeless good humor and wonderful opportunities for virtuoso singing. Figaro's aria, *"Largo al factotum"* ("Make way for the factotum of the city"), ranks with the most popular baritone songs of all time, and Rosina's *"Una voce poco fa"* (The voice I heard just now"), elicits spontaneous applause today—more than 150 years after its first performance.

The ebullient overture has little to do with the story of *The Barber*. Presumedly, Rossini was as careless as he was facile—he misplaced the original and substituted one he had written for *Elizabeth*.

At its first performances, Rosina was sung by a contralto. Later, coloratura sopranos took it over. Today, with gifted singers in both categories, audiences are treated to both versions.

La Gazza Ladra (*The Thieving Magpie*) followed in 1817, and Rossini's next success was *La Cenerentola* (*Cinderella*) the same year. His version of the famous fairy tale bounces from one melodic tune to another, and the title role is sung by a mezzo or contralto.

His last Italian opera was *Semiramide,* written in 1823. It, like two other operas, *Mosè in Egitto* (*Moses in Egypt*) and *La Donna del Lago* (*Lady of the Lake*), marks Rossini's several attempts to dispense with comic opera and write in a dramatic style.

He settled in Paris, in 1824, and his *Le Comte d'Ory* (*Count Ory*) (1828) made it obvious that he was capable of writing a true *opéra comique*. *Guillaume Tell* (*William Tell*) (1829) was the last opera he wrote, and it is a superb realization of genuine nineteenth-century grand opera. It was critically acclaimed, but the public never responded to it. At thirty-seven, the composer who could proudly claim that twenty-three of his operas were being performed at one time throughout the world, decided to forget the theater. There are those who believe that the Revolution of 1830 and Louis-Philippe's ascent to the French throne made Rossini realize that his days as a celebrity might be numbered. The new king admired only Grétry's music, and Meyerbeer was skyrocketing to fame. Rossini himself claimed that he was running out of melodies. His home became his theater, so to speak. He was surrounded by musicians and writers, he became a renowned gourmet, an infallible judge of foods and wine, and he remained a brilliant wit for the rest of his life. Before he died he composed only two works of note: his *Stabat Mater* and his *Petite messe solennelle*.

Rossini was seventy-six when he died, and he had watched both the spectacular rise of Meyerbeer and grand opera *and* the fall of his beloved *opera buffa*. With his wit and his intelligence (and his bitter melancholia) he probably philosophized that he had taken it to a mountaintop from which there was no place to go but down.

Gaetano Donizetti (1797–1848) composed like a demon. His list of seventy-three operas is only a part of the music he put to paper during his lifetime. He, like Rossini, had two special gifts—a perceptive ear for limitless melody (and the talent to write it) plus an extraordinary ability to write coloratura. All of his heroines require sopranos with skyrocket techniques as well as beautiful voices.

Donizetti's first major opera was *Anna Bolena* (1830). *L'elisir d'amore* (*The Elixir of Love*) (1832), a romantic comedy about an amorous young couple and mysterious love potions, has been a perennial favorite since its first performance. Its creamy, lyrical tenor aria, *"Una furtiva lagrima"* ("A furtive tear"), is a prime example of Donizetti's uncanny talent for writing tunes that stay with the listener long after he has left the theater.

He followed this comedy with a—for his time—violent, romantic opera about one of history's most violent and romantic figures, Lucrezia Borgia. It was premiered at Milan's famous La Scala in 1833. Wicked or not, *Lucrezia Borgia,* with all her lovely melodies, found it difficult to survive the test of time until the Spanish soprano, Monserrat Caballé, sang the title role on the evening of her American debut in 1965. Since then Miss Caballé has taken Lucrezia and her poisons to major opera houses all over the world. *Lucia di Lammermoor* was first given in Naples in 1835. Many accept this opera as the composer's best. Since its premiere, hundreds of coloraturas have valiantly and hopefully soared through the flute-ridden pitfalls of *Lucia's* mad scene in the third act. *Lucia* is also famous and memorable for the great sextet that demands superb singers in each of the vocal parts if one is to hear how unusually gifted Donizetti was at creating emotion and character study through his music.

Donizetti was a great favorite in Paris and his *La fille du régiment* (*The Daughter of the Regiment*) and *La Favorite* (*The Favorite Lady*) (to French texts) were written expressly for theaters there. *Don Pasquale* (1843), a delightful comic opera, is full of fun and melody, and the music dances through the comic antics that involve an aging bachelor's being outwitted by the young and beautiful Norina and her youthful lover.

Vincenzo Bellini was born in Sicily in 1801. He died thirty-four years later, and of his several operas only three are performed today. Bellini, as a person and a musician, was more introspective than Donizetti and Rossini. He was a composer of elegance and capable of creating heartrendingly beautiful melodies. *Il Pirata* (*The Pirate*) in 1827 was a modest success in Milan, but his next work, *La Sonnambula* (*The Sleepwalker*), set him up as a musician with qualifications for international success. The sentimental tale about a lovely girl whose sleepwalking tendencies involve her in village slander (and almost deprive her of her true love) is saved more than once by the touching melodies alloted to the heroine, Amina. The longlined and melancholy soprano aria, *"Ah! non credea"* ("I hadn't thought I'd see you"), can bring tears to one's eyes—if it is sung by an artist. Almost all of Bellini's operas depended on the ability of singers to sing slow coloratura. The command of slow coloratura requires superhuman control. Nineteenth-century serious opera never expected the coloratura passages to be dashed off at an electrifying tempo; or that they would be sung by the high, fluty voices that we are accustomed to today. Composers wrote these passages to be sung by a heavier voice, at a slower speed. And they were to be interpreted with dramatic expression.

The question arises as to whatever became of these dramatic coloraturas. More accurately we should call such a singer a dramatic soprano *d'agilità,* a dramatic female voice with great flexibility. Placing singers, sopranos especially, into categories of light, lyric, or dramatic began a half century or so ago. When the *castrati* disappeared, composers, including Rossini and Bellini, began writing for the female voice. Some of the women with natural contralto voices were able, with scrupulous training, to extend their range. In other words, they added notes to the tops of their voices that enabled them to sing soprano roles as well. Maria Malibran was this type of singer.

In early nineteenth-century opera a soprano role was written for a soprano. Never in his wildest imagination did a composer dream of writing for a lyric, a dramatic, or a coloratura voice. A soprano was *all* of them. The truth is that Bellini wrote both *La Sonnambula* and *Norma* for the same voice. Milanese Giuditta Pasta was the first soprano to sing them. Malibran was also an interpreter of both heroines. In recent years, only the great Maria Callas has had the technique, the voice, and the understanding of style to run this gamut. Callas, who is a true soprano *d'agilità,* was born in New York City (1923) of Greek parents. Her first professional appearance was at the age of sixteen, in Athens. The work was von Suppé's *Boccaccio.*

With the advance of Meyerbeerian opera in France, and with the Italians who followed suit, a division of soprano voices appeared. One soprano was given nothing but bravura music to sing and another nothing but dramatic passages. Opera audiences were confronted with the dramatic and the coloratura species as we hear them today.

The romantic ideas and frail heroines of Bellini and Donizetti gave way to earthier passions and flesh-and-blood people. As a new style of dramatic singing increased, the earlier type of singer ceased to exist. Since there was no longer a need for immaculately trained voices—ones that could sing anything with emotion and subtle coloring—but more of a demand for dramatic enunciation and, most of all, a need of power to sustain the volume over the increasingly large orchestras, the true interpreters of Rossini, Bellini, and Donizetti disappeared.

With the meteoric appearance of Maria Callas in the 1950s, European and American audiences were able to hear for the first time what these extraordinary sopranos had sounded like. Not only did her versatility and her theatrical imagination allow her to encompass all these fabulous roles, she sang them as they must have been sung at the time of their creation. Among other things, she was able to return to the authentic style—with its perilous demands for slow coloratura. Contemporary ears, attuned to rapid, glittering vocal displays by endearing coloraturas could not believe their ears. Some still do not understand the art of Maria Callas.

Norma (1831) is one of Bellini's greatest successes, and it contains one of the most beautiful and taxing arias in all opera, *"Casta diva"* ("Chaste Goddess"). Another American singer, Rosa Ponselle, has become a part of music history by way of her interpretation of this demanding role. When *Norma* was revived at the Metropolitan in 1927—for Miss Ponselle—the role of her father, Oroveso, was sung by Ezio Pinza. Later he would take the country by storm—in *South Pacific*.

Melody and the power of song were of major importance to each of these distinctly Italian composers. They also realized that their melodies could be enhanced by dramatic expressivity, and this, with their additions of new orchestral sounds and rhythms, opened important doors for opera. Their works live on.

Callas has opened a few doors also. She has made it possible for audiences and new singers to investigate and succumb to the glorious beauties of romantic Italian opera.

We thank all four of them.

Giuseppe Verdi

Richard Wagner

Georges Bizet

Giacomo Puccini

Richard Strauss

Leonard Bernstein

Benjamin Britten

The Bettmann Archive

Samuel Barber

Maria Jeritza

Amelita Galli-Curci

Mary Garden

Enrico Caruso

Lauritz Melchior

Metropolitan Opera Archives

Giovanni Martinelli

Chaliapin

Marian Anderson   *Metropolitan Opera Archives*

Regina Resnik

Leontyne Price

Renata Tebaldi

Maria Callas   *Paolo Costa/Angel Records*

Carmen

Aida

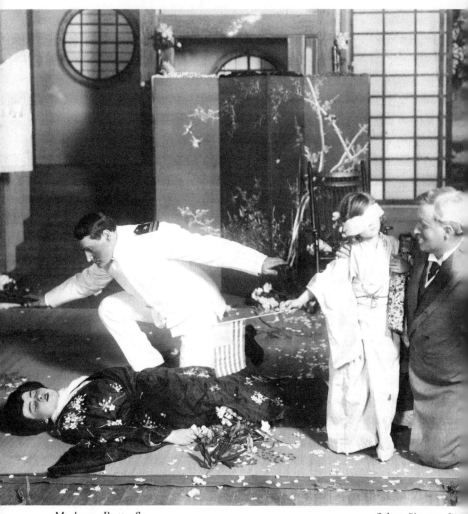

Madame Butterfly

Il Trovator

The Medium

Electra

The Ballad of Baby Doe

Der Rosenkavalier

Boris Godunov   *The Bettmann Archive*

Tosca

The Girl of the Golden West   *The Bettmann Archive*

My Fair Lady

The Barber of Seville

All the World's a Joke

Giuseppe Verdi (1813–1901) was born in a dangerous time and a dangerous place. Le Roncole, Italy, Verdi's birthplace, was suffering under Napoleon's dreams of empire. Her people continued to suffer when the "liberating" Austrian troops accused them of siding with the French and set about to destroy the village. Giuseppe's mother hid herself and her son in the tower of Le Roncole's church and managed to save her own life and that of the boy who was destined to become one of the great masters of opera.

His proud parents did their utmost to see that his musical talents were fulfilled. At fifteen his compositions for festivals and special occasions in the town of Busseto brought him to the attention of several businessmen who got together enough money for him to go to Milan for advanced study.

Verdi did not impress the sophisticated Milanese. In fact, he wasn't allowed to enter the famous Conservatory there because he was too old. He was eighteen!

It was the school's loss. He met a prompter who was on the

staff of the magnificent La Scala opera house and the gentleman became his teacher and his devoted friend. Quite by accident, Verdi substituted for an ailing conductor at a presentation of Haydn's *The Creation,* and his polished performance
gained him an offer to write an opera. This first opera, *Oberto,*
was jinxed. Rehearsals were canceled constantly, and then its
leading tenor took sick. Only the interference of soprano Giu-
seppina Strepponi finally straightened things out so that his
work had a premiere at all. The opening night response, November 17, 1839, was grim. But the young composer was con-
tracted to write three more operas.

His marriage and short life with Margherita Barezzi was itself a tragic libretto. The two children of that marriage died
within two years, and Margherita died while he was writing
his second opera, *Un giorno di regno* or *Il finto Stanislao*
(*Stanislaus,* or *The Pretender's Day of Power*). Verdi never
had any empathy for this *buffa opera* and, plagued as he was
with heartbreak and tragedy, one can easily imagine why it
was not destined to be a "hit." He swore that he would never
write another note of music.

He retired to Busseto where he brooded and found life unbearable. Back in Milan, he gave way to a suggestion from La
Scala's manager, Bartolemeo Merelli, that he set a story about
the tyrannical Nebuchadnezzar and the suffering Jews to
music. Its dramatic biblical narrative was exactly what Verdi
needed at this moment in his life—and his career. He had
reached the decision that he and his music were going to be a
part of the new Italy—an Italy that must rise out of the ashes
of war and occupation to a united freedom she had never
known.

The Italians were quick to recognize the calls to freedom in *Nabucco* (1842), and they responded as only Italians can. They pounced on its blazing patriotism and its dramatic music and acclaimed the opera with cries of *"Viva Verdi!"*

Strepponi was back in his life again. The brilliant soprano sang the leading role of Abigaille. Subsequently she retired to become Verdi's companion—and later his wife. In 1843, *I Lombardi alla prima Crociata* (*The Lombards at the First Crusade*) survived efforts of the police to stop its first performance, and its thrilling success with the masses made Verdi a national hero. Venice commissioned him to write an opera for its dignified Teatro Fenice, and he presented *Ernani*. The libretto is based on a fiery play by Victor Hugo, and one of its soprano arias, *"Ernani involami"* ("Ernani, take me away"), is still a favorite with audiences and singers.

Florence, in 1847, was the scene of his new opera, *Macbeth*. Verdi had always lacked discernment in choosing his librettos (and librettists), and *Macbeth* was subjected to the same plight. Shakespeare was, and always would be, a great favorite of Verdi's, and although this opera does capture some of the chilling, bloody drama of the play, there is little doubt that it could have been a far greater success if its libretto had been first class.

Luisa Miller, based on a play by Schiller, was premiered at the San Carlo Theater, Naples, in 1849, and *Rigoletto*—one of the most popular operas of all time—was presented in 1851.

It was not the first—nor the last—time that Verdi was to be in trouble with the censors. Victor Hugo's play, *Le Roi s'amuse* (*The King Amuses Himself*), a melodrama that Parisian censors had banned because of its political innuendos and its lecherous characters, was just the provocative material that could inspire a man like Verdi. He composed the opera in forty days!

The title role is a tour de force for great dramatic baritones. The opera itself marks the first time that Verdi really attempted to escape from the Italian idea that opera has to offer the public successive vocal "numbers" strung together without any thought-provoking complications from the music that connects them. In *Rigoletto* everything is of one piece. Even the show-stopping arias—*"Questa o quella"* ("This One or That One, It's All the Same to Me") for the tenor, *"Caro nome"* ("Beloved Name") the soprano's haunting declaration of first love, and the world famous quartet of the last act—are born of the dramatic action, and every phrase leads naturally to the next emotional involvement.

All of *Rigoletto's* arias, especially the tenor's *"La Donna è Mobile"* ("Woman Is Fickle") have been accused (as have many of Verdi's operas at one time or another) of being maudlin and smacking of organ-grinder sounds. When sung by serious artists, and as Verdi intended them to be sung, they are valid and very often touching.

* Rome's famous river, the Tiber, decided to overflow its banks at the time arranged for Verdi's next premiere. But it took more than mud and water to keep the determined Romans from being present at the Maestro's newest success, *Il Trovatore (The Troubadour)* (1853). If one is strong and refuses to be sidetracked by its incredible and complicated plot by a Spanish playwright, Antonio Gutierrez, one realizes the score is full of thrilling arias and duets.

Verdi's preoccupation with the expression of human passions

through melody and the voice is abundantly apparent in *Il Trovatore*. Psychological motivations and nebulous philosophies play no part in his songs. *"Ai nostri monti"* ("Home to Our Mountains"), the somber and beautiful duet for tenor and mezzo, in the last act, is typical of Verdi's ability to get to the heart of human emotions. The gypsy Azucena, and her foster son, Manrico, imprisoned and waiting for death, calmly and nostalgically sing of returning to their former life with such heartfelt and eloquent Verdian simplicity that one cannot help but be moved.

It is difficult to believe, but, six weeks after the first sensational success of *Il Trovatore,* another Verdi opera appeared. It was called *La Traviata.*

La Traviata was based on Alexandre Dumas' *La Dame aux Camélias* (*The Lady of the Camellias*), and the heroine of both the opera and the play can be easily recognized as the ill-fated, real-life courtesan, Mlle du Plessis.

An obese and far from attractive soprano who sang Violetta at the first performance, failing to create any image of the gorgeous but not so moral young lady, had much to do with the audience's being unwilling to accept the opera. Happily, she was replaced, and now *La Traviata* is a signal for "standing room only" at opera houses around the world.

The musical style of *La Traviata* is sensuously intimate, and Verdi's use of soft, caressing strings in the overture and in the sad, romantic prelude to the third act subtly captures the air of romantic frustration and death that hovers over the opera.

Violetta has two arias, *"Ah, fors' è lui"* ("Perhaps it is for him that my soul is waiting"), with its glittering finale

"Sempre libera" ("Always free"), and her *"Addio del passato"* ("Farewell to the Past"), that are perfect examples of Verdi's uncanny ability to write emotional character studies—all the time displaying the beauty of the human voice.

La Traviata is romantic realism in opera at its very best. It was also a turning point in Verdi's creativity. He suddenly realized how effectively he could underplay—both musically and dramatically.

Now Verdi's theatrical successes and his increasing power as a political figure had established him as an international celebrity whom even brittle Paris could not ignore. His *Les Vêpres Siciliennes* (*Sicilian Vespers*) (1855) was applauded for fifty performances in the French capital. It cannot be said that Italian audiences reacted as warmly. Nor did they to *Simon Boccanegra* in 1857. Failures have been known to travel in threes and this was such an instance. *Aroldo,* several months later, was a fiasco, too.

The censors in Naplês stepped in again to aggravate the production of his next opera, *Un Ballo in Maschera* (*A Masked Ball*) (1859). Verdi adamantly refused to water down the libretto (the authorities were convinced that its political overtones and the assassination of its leading character were overt displays of hatred for the ruling power), and he took the opera to Rome. There, the censors were as dogmatic as the Neapolitans. Reluctantly, Verdi changed the nationality of his characters and set the locale in Boston!

La Forza del Destino (*The Force of Destiny*) was written for the Imperial Theater of St. Petersburg, but it might as well have been performed in Siberia for all the enthusiasm it generated. Later, opera lovers in Spain responded in a manner that seems typical of audiences today; they loved the melodies, particularly *"Pace, pace, mio Dio"*("Peace, Peace, My God") for the leading soprano, and ignored the gloomy plot. *Don Carlos* (1867) was written for the elegant Paris Opéra, and Verdi sincerely intended it to be Meyerbeerian. The censors didn't figure in the difficulties this time—anti-Italian feelings in France did. At its premiere, the glamorous Empress Eugénie publicly showed her disapproval of the opera's theme. All of Paris and the critics followed suit, and this combination of reactions plus Verdi's melancholy left him dejected and despondent. He retired again.

Two years later a project was brought to his attention that was to develop into one of his greatest creations. *Aïda* had many things in its favor. The libretto was a passionate drama set in ancient Egypt; it was to be produced for a history-making occasion, the opening of the Suez Canal; and Verdi was to receive 150,000 francs for composing it. The Franco-Prussian War delayed *Aïda*'s scheduled premiere for almost a year, but December 24, 1871, was a red-letter day for opera. From the moment its hero, Radames, sings *"Celeste Aïda"* ("Celestial Aida"), the opera pours out a torrent of melody and pageantry. The soprano aria, *"Ritorna vincitor!"* ("Return Victorious"), the spectacle of the triumphal march scene, and the beauties of the Nile scene are mere suggestions of the glories that enrich this eternally popular grand opera.

If Verdi had not written another note, *Aïda* would be proof that he was in full command of his gifts of harmony, melody, orchestration, and his knowledge of the human voice.

At sixty, he was wealthy, popular, and successful. His silence during the years that followed convinced some that his gifts for melody had been drained dry. For thirteen years he wrote nothing but the tremendous Manzoni *Requiem*. Then, because of the serious concern of friends, the composer was brought into contact with Arrigo Boïto!

Boïto is remembered chiefly as being probably the greatest librettist in history. He was also a composer of merit, and two of his operas, *Mefistofele* and *Nerone,* have achieved great success, particularly in Italy. He believed that great music demanded great words, and his libretto for *Otello* proves that he was right.

The collaboration of Boïto and Verdi culminated in a masterpiece. In 1887, when Verdi was seventy-four, *Otello*'s first performance proved to audiences and critics alike that the genius of Verdi was still alive—alive with a strength and imagination that would have put many a younger man to shame.

At eighty, he was as tireless in his outpouring of music as he had been in his fight for freedom. He and Boïto finished *Falstaff*. In 1893, the dogmatic Italian whose operatic successes and failures, as well as his life, had been clothed in gloomy tragedy presented the world with his last opera. It was a brilliant comedy.

Gone were the obvious and sometimes vulgar melodies. Forgotten were the days when the organ grinder had tantalized him in Le Roncole. Throughout its seamless, warm-hearted, laughing score nothing is too much—or too little. Everything is right.

Despite the loneliness that came with growing older, Maestro Verdi proved with *Falstaff* that he was blessed with the youthful ability to laugh. One of his letters explains: "I wrote it for fun."

Perhaps it is *Falstaff*'s sophisticated craftsmanship, its perfection, that has kept it the prime example—for musicians, critics, and artists—of *opera buffa*. But what of the public? They prefer its competitors: *The Barber of Seville, The Marriage of Figaro* and *The Mastersingers*.

Maestro Verdi would have agreed with Falstaff:

"All the world's a joke."

CHAPTER ELEVEN

I Can Still Hear the Singers! Wagner and Strauss

Richard Wagner (1813–1883) had the mad King Ludwig of Bavaria as his mentor, and there are those who consider Wagner something of a madman himself. In addition to being a composer, history has categorized him as a racial propagandist, a socialist, an anti-Semite, a Jungian, and an indulgent egoist. But friend and foe alike agree that he was a genius. One may loathe his operas, but they can never be denied.

Richard Wagner was born in Leipzig, Germany, on May 22, 1813. In November his father died, and an actor, Ludwig Geyer, stepped in to become head of the family. Geyer died when Richard was eight, and although it has not been proved, it has been suggested by many (including Wagner himself) that Geyer was possibly his real father.

Richard greatly admired Geyer, whether he was his father or not, and it is certain that the man instilled in the boy a wild love of anything connected with the theater. As a student and as a personality, Richard hated form of any kind. Early in life he wrote that form—as educators tried to sell it in schools and textbooks—was a sword without a blade.

He was a morbid child and talked and wrote unsparingly about how he was influenced by Beethoven, E. T. A. Hoffmann, and the inspired singing of Schröder-Devrient, whom he heard singing *Fidelio* when he was sixteen.

At college (and for all his life) he was a hotheaded reactionary. He was convinced that he was destined to be a revolutionary composer. The public wasn't so sure. His hardly memorable early works were rarely played, and in order to keep from starving (and to keep supplied with champagne), he took a job as a conductor in Magdeburg. There he acquired a sizable amount of knowledge about techniques of orchestration and the ideal collaboration of orchestra and singer. He also wrote an opera, *Das Liebesverbot (The Ban on Love)* (1836), with a libretto that owed much to Shakespeare's *Measure for Measure*. Wagner's version naïvely attempted to do away with long-accepted behavior patterns and moral codes. Perhaps he was the first "flower child."

Following a frustrating courtship, he married an actress, Wilhelmina (Minna) Planer, and in between their violent arguments he continued his experimental forays into the combination of music and drama.

He was much impressed with Bellini's gift for melody and confessed that it was his "zeal and fervor for Italian opera" that succeeded in getting him his position as conductor at Riga's Opera House. The intendant (general manager), Holtei, programmed "the lighter, more frivolous music."

Wagner's dreams of grandeur were not compatible with this frivolous climate, and before long he found that he was not indispensable. He was fired.

He and Minna—and their Newfoundland, Robber—headed

for Paris, by way of London. A chance meeting with the influential Meyerbeer netted Wagner important papers of introduction, and Richard and Minna stormed the capital of France
with high spirits. The French lost little time in alerting them
to reality. For a couple of years Minna was occupied with running a boarding house and keeping her husband out of jail. All
the while he was completing an opera, *Rienzi,* which he had
started in Dresden. The King of Saxony was impressed with
the music and promised it a hearing. So, with new energy and
courage, Wagner also finished *Der fliegende Holländer* (*The
Flying Dutchman*) and sent it on to Berlin.

Rienzi (1842) was a success, due to its star soprano,
Schröder-Devrient, and a magnificent tenor in the title role.

If he was imitating Meyerbeer, Wagner was supremely successful. The opera is BIG—with big choral effects, big theatrical sounds, a grandiose prayer for the tenor-hero, and little
depth.

The Flying Dutchman (1843) didn't fare so well. The Dresden audience appeared to be willing to try to like the new
opera, but the singers were distressingly confused about everything they were doing and completely blank as to what Wagner was trying to achieve. The evening was a disaster. Operagoers in Berlin liked *The Dutchman,* but the critics cut it to
pieces. Twenty-five years elapsed before it was heard again.
The Dutchman is important because it demonstrates what extraordinary steps Wagner was taking in his search for the ideal
—completely unbroken music and dramatic action. Stylisti-
cally, it is a Wagnerian effort to use all that he had found admirable in Weber. And, like *Der Freischütz,* the opera evolves
around the dynamic forces of nature and the supernatural.

This opera also focuses our attention on another Wagnerian ideal—his obsession with the idea of redemption through great love. This theme is firmly set into this and all his future music dramas.

Wagner's *Tannhäuser* (1845) tells the story of a thirteenth-century knight who forsakes the noble Elisabeth for Venus, the voluptuous goddess of love. *Tannhäuser* has many remarkably melodic scenes and arias, including the song to the evening star, the ever-popular pilgrims' chorus, and the paganly erotic Venusberg ballet music. This exciting scene, much to the dismay of the opera manager, was written by Wagner to be performed in the first act. The head of the Opera knew that the Jockey Club, a group of effete and wealthy young opera buffs, never arrived at the theater until the first act was ending. If they discovered that the expected ballet was over, they would probably cause a riot. They did. *Tannhäuser* was one of the great first-night catastrophes of all time.

Courageous sopranos have been known to sing both Venus and Elisabeth in the same performance. It should be noted that not even the superb Swedish soprano, Birgit Nilsson, was able to carry off the feat with genuine conviction at her recent Metropolitan Opera performances.

Wagner, who conceived all of his music dramas before he was forty, completed his medieval fairy tale *Lohengrin* (1848) just before his thirty-fifth birthday. The music for the Holy Grail theme—first heard in the lovely prelude—is a perfect example of Wagner's increasingly powerful use of leitmotivs. A leitmotiv is a leading motive. The term was created by F. W. Jähns to describe a brief musical passage that identifies an idea or a person in opera. Its origins are not certain although the idea was used by Gluck, Mozart, and Weber. Leitmotiv was a Wagnerian obsession.

Lohengrin, with its dreamlike, religious mood, its majestic knights, the evil Ortrud, and the magic swan boat, can be an impressive spectacle. Lohengrin's arrival and departure in his swan boat have been known to cause some frantic moments. Walter Slezak tells of the time when his father, Leo, one of the greatest operatic tenors, was singing *Lohengrin,* and the swan departed into the wings without him. He commented—*sotto voce*—to his colleagues on stage: "What time does the next swan leave?"

One need never to have stepped inside an opera house to be familiar with *Lohengrin*'s world famous wedding march.

Four great music dramas, *Das Rheingold* (*The Rhine Gold*) *Die Walküre* (*The Valkyrie*), *Siegfried,* and *Die Götterdämmerung* (*The Twilight of the Gods*), are known as the *Ring* cycle or *Der Ring des Nibelungen* (*The Ring of the Nibelungs*). They were composed over a period of twenty-one years (1853–1874). The leading motives of the gods, giants, love, and redemption are woven in miraculous detail throughout the four dramas that explain the history of the Rhine gold. The *Ring* is the accepted short title for the Nibelungs' Ring, a series of German legends, which told of a great mass of gold which was stolen from the Rhine maidens. It was later fashioned into a magic ring, and its first possessor was Alberich, one of the Nibelung race of dwarfs.

All these music dramas, as well as *Tristan* and *Isolde,* which was first given in Munich (1865), exemplify many of the extraordinary ideas Wagner brought to opera and to future composers.

He started, and insisted upon, the practice that the theater be darkened before the performance was allowed to begin. He justifiably believed that bright lights in the auditorium work against the mood of the music.

He wrote for large orchestras and made his orchestra *one* with all of the characters in his music dramas.

No composer has achieved more than he did with polyphonic melody. Polyphony literally means a simultaneous sounding of notes. However, it also implies the use of counterpoint (one melody being spoken in counterpoint to another).

He refused to cater to singers. They, the chorus, the orchestra, the settings—everything was a part of his overall canvas of music. The song, the drama, the orchestra moved along without interruption.

His demands were musical, poetic, and theatrical. Wagnerian singers must have abundant physical and mental stamina to sustain every Wagnerian performance.

Wagner's operas demand heroic voices and heroic singers who can sing with (and over) a tremendous orchestra for as long as four hours—quite a contrast to heroes and heroines of some Puccini operas who—if the notes and arias were put end to end—sing twenty or thirty minutes during the performance.

It was a memorable day for Wagner and the Metropolitan Opera when Kirsten Flagstad made her first appearance in New York. The Norwegian soprano was planning to retire in the 1930s when she was asked to sing for the Metropolitan. She was a sensation, and her performances made Wagner a new, box-office commodity, thereby saving the opera house almost singlehandedly from a gloomy financial period.

One of her greatest roles was Isolde in *Tristan und Isolde.*

Wagner based his dramatic poem for this music drama on one of the many legends surrounding the court of King Arthur.

It is one of the truly great love dramas, and in it Wagner makes his primary belief—that great passion cannot be consummated—quite clear. Death, he also believed, is the ultimate goal of passion because passion survives only under impossible conditions. Tristan and Isolde, who believe they hate each other, drink a magic potion thinking it will bring them death. The potion is a symbol of the two characters' true recognition and desire for release.

With repeated hearings, one can recognize that Wagner's orchestra in *Tristan* interprets the *psychological*—his characters on the stage interpret everything that is felt.

In *The Ring of the Nibelungs* Wagner concentrates on the mystical power of greed—not passion. *The Rhine Gold* is a prologue that explains how gold was stolen from the Rhine maidens and prophesies that its possession is a guarantee of destruction and death. In *The Valkyrie* we meet Wotan, the greatest of the mythical gods, his daughter Brünnhilde, and the parents of the hero of the *Ring,* Siegfried. The final drama, *Die Götterdämmerung,* ends with more of Wagner's impressive musical moralizing—that love, never money or power, conquers the universe.

Authorities on Wagner and his music have listed some two hundred different leitmotivs in the *Ring.* Wagner introduces, elaborates upon, and discusses each one musically until he is certain that it is firmly implanted in the listener's memory. Then, hopefully, the motifs will stay with the listener to assist him in following and taking part in the many moral and dramatic ideas that glow and burst into flame throughout the four dramas.

Die Meistersinger von Nürnberg (*The Mastersingers of Nuremberg*) (1868) is a comic masterpiece. It was written during a time when Wagner was free of financial harassments, thanks to the lavish patronage of the Bavarian king, Ludwig II.

The young lovers of the story, Walther and Eva, are beautifully characterized examples of youth's impatience and eagerness. And Hans Sachs, the wise, old gentleman who makes the people of Nuremberg understand that the old must make way for the new is a unique operatic portrait. Wagner's musical fabric for *Die Meistersinger,* from the opening bars of the magnificent overture to the inspiring finale, clothes the story and the characters in a variety of living colors. Its characters are people —not larger-than-life symbols—who are involved in human failings and ambitions. Combine romance, stuffy traditionalism, impetuous youth, dogmatic maturity, and the genuine need of all civilized mankind for the truth of art, and you have the elements that make this human comedy an enduring masterpiece.

Actual human failing and real romance surrounded the creation of *Die Meistersinger*. Cosima, the twenty-six-year-old wife of Hans von Bülow, the conductor of the opera's first performance, deserted her husband to join Wagner in Switzerland. But the scandal involving the three of them subsided gradually, and the premiere on June 21, 1868, was a tremendous popular success. The press was, as usual, less impressed.

All of Wagner's music dramas required great scenic productions, and to assure that they would be presented in definitive

surroundings, Wagner decided that he must have his own theater. The Bavarians, enraged over their King's mad expendi-
tures of money in the composer's behalf, called a halt. However, Wagner organizations all over the world came to the
composer's rescue, and in 1876 the Festival Theater in Bayreuth opened its doors to one of the most elegant audiences in
music history.

It remains today, despite its back-breakingly uncomfortable
wooden seats, one of the theater wonders of the world. The orchestra pit is not visible to the audience, and its lid affords the
balance of sound Wagner felt was imperative for the realization of his music dramas. The first complete *Ring* comprised
the opening performances of the Festival Theater. It might
have been interesting to see how the stage designers and producers of 1876, without electricity and with Wagner's demands
for "naturalistic" settings, brought his dramas to life.

It is certain that the first *Göterdämmerung* Brünnhilde,
Amalie Materna, did not jump on the back of her horse,
Grane, and leap into a flaming pyre as the beautiful Australian
soprano Marjorie Lawrence did in the late 1930s.

It is also suspect that Richard Wagner would have agreed to
the scenic changes his music dramas would be subjected to in
the hands of his grandson, Wieland. Wieland produced all of
his grandfather's works at the Bayreuth Festival from the time
of its reopening in 1951 until his death in 1966.

Wieland's productions caused much controversy, mainly because he practiced what he preached—that opera must be produced in the style of the times. Specifically, he claimed that a
style that was right for opera in 1938 was not right for 1958—
and it simply would not do for 1968. He aimed at making

opera significant for audiences of the moment. "Definitive" was not a word in his vocabulary—everything is subject to change. He conceived his grandfather's *Ring* cycle as music drama that dealt with something greater than German mythology. He visualized the *Ring* as theater in the classic Greek style. This classic idea necessitated that he use a simple, atmospheric stage—one not burdened with unnecessary, realistic detail. In his own words, he wanted to create "mythical dream-pictures." He believed that his grandfather died ten years before he had the opportunity of collaborating with a scenic designer whose stature and imagination were equal to Wagner's music. Wieland was a master of stage lighting. He used bold lighting effects to replace old-fashioned scenery, and he did away with old-fashioned gestures that signified nothing but movement for movement's sake. He was searching for a visual, as well as a musical, way of expressing the truths he was convinced were a part of all opera. Perhaps the composer of *Die Meistersinger* would have conceded to his grandson's point— the old must make way for the new—not just for the newness and novelty of being different, but because truth must be expressed in contemporary terms.

A year before Richard Wagner died, the public heard his last work, *Parsifal* (1882). Debussy called *Parsifal* a "beautiful monument of sound raised to the true glory of music." Others have called it a monument of senility and an intolerable bore. Due to its religious, festival-play story that takes place on Good Friday, Wagner's ponderous music drama is generally performed at Eastertime.

In 1883 Wagner died. All of his works and the Festival Theater in Bayreuth came under the domineering and implacable control of Cosima. In a scene that must have reminded some of the famous love death in *Tristan and Isolde,* Wagner's wife cut her hair and laid it on her husband's dead body. Death made her the mistress of a cult and a musical Valhalla. She ruled it until 1930, never suspecting that Wagner was not, and had never been, a god.

Richard Strauss (1864–1949) was the son of a musician who had played in orchestras under the baton of Richard Wagner.

Franz Strauss accused Wagner and his music of being degenerate, little suspecting how future audiences and critics would label his son's creations "shocking." Young Richard was well educated, and while he was in his teens he composed many orchestral pieces including a symphony that brought him to the attention of the renowned conductor Hermann Levi.

Another conductor, von Bülow (of the aforementioned Cosima-Wagner scandal) was also deeply impressed by the boy's talents and made him his assistant. When von Bülow retired, Strauss became the chief conductor of the Meiningen Orchestra. It was during his tenure there that he came under the influence of Alexander Ritter, a musician and devotee of the daringly "new" music of that time. Strauss forsook his original classic ambitions and dashed headlong down the roads paved by Wagner and Berlioz. He attempted to emulate Wagner, not only musically but by writing his own libretto for his first opera, *Guntram* (1894). Its failure was responsible for his achieving fame and financial success by way of another form —the symphonic tone poem.

Seven years later, with his ego boosted, he wrote *Feuersnot* (*The Fire Famine*) (1901). Its libretto was considered vulgar and ribald at that time, and the whole affair seems to have been a way for Strauss to take a few public jabs at the hated Munich critics who had been less than friendly to both him and Wagner.

In 1903, his unimaginative *Sinfonia domestica* (*Domestic Symphony*) convinced his admirers as well as his enemies that he had written himself out at the age of thirty-nine. No one was prepared for his next move. A play by Oscar Wilde, *Salome,* with its petulant and perverse teen-age seductress of biblical legend, was a fashionable success throughout Germany. It was the ideal libretto for Strauss.

Its "shocking" story and its more "shocking" music made Strauss an overnight sensation. German opera audiences clamored for it, and the perennial moralists insisted that the work be banned. What better way to make the music world pay attention? London operagoers demanded a hearing of the bizarre and difficult work. The censors refused. New Yorkers fared somewhat better. The decadent little girl managed to survive one performance before the staid management, puritan subscribers, and offended newspapermen forced her off the stage. *Salome* returned to New York in 1909 as a vehicle for the unique Mary Garden at the Manhattan Opera House. Her brilliant acting and singing plus Strauss's craftily planned "striptease"—the Dance of the Seven Veils—made music history. Squeamish Metropolitan audiences had to accept a red scarf in place of the head of John the Baptist (in the final scene) for many years. That is, until the exciting Bulgarian soprano, Ljuba Welitsch, electrified New Yorkers with her stunning performances in 1949. The faint of heart were still fighting the wicked child, though. The management suggested that

Miss Welitsch's exposure of nudity might be too much. She explained that her interpretation was historically valid, and *Salome* was finally accepted as a powerful and important musical work.

Critics and audiences were convinced that *Elektra* (1909) was merely the crafty Strauss's new attempt to shock. They were wrong. Strauss and his librettist, Hugo von Hofmannstahl, had created a monumental musical tragedy.

Elektra requires an orchestra of 110 musicians and singers of inhuman strength. The great contralto, Ernestine Schumann-Heink, who created the role of Klytämnestra, refused to sing more than one performance of the work. It is said that she heard Strauss screaming at the conductor during the rehearsals: "Louder, louder with the orchestra! I can still hear Schumann-Heink!"

Elektra created another sensation in New York when the Philharmonic Symphony presented the work (1937)—in a concert version—with Rosa Pauly in the title role. Pauly's dramatic singing of the opera swept everything before it. Her incredible voice and her intensity surmounted all the complexities of the score and won her a standing ovation of several minutes' duration—an event that will never be forgotten by those fortunate enough to hear it.

Considering that Strauss was deeply impressed with money, he must have been pleased to know that his fees from his publisher had increased from $15,000 for his shocking *Salome* to $27,000 for *Elektra*—plus the tidy sum of $18,000 in advance for the American rights to the latter work!

In 1908 the Berlin Opera appointed him its director. And in 1911 the world was anxiously waiting for a new work from the pen of one of the world's most famous and financially successful operatic composers.

His next opera, *Der Rosenkavalier* (*The Rose Cavalier*) (1911), was a complete turnabout from the gloom and despair of *Elektra*. It is a comic opera, sparkling with waltzes, Viennese chivalry, young love, and approaching middle age. All of its characters, Oktavian, Sophie, Baron Ochs, and the beautiful Marschallin are compassionate and understandable human beings.

The inimitable German soprano, Lotte Lehmann, was one of Strauss's favorite singers, and to this day no other soprano has really erased memories of her portrait of the Marschallin. The closing scene of the first act is one of the most touching in all opera. The Marschallin sits at her dressing table and looks into its baroque, gold mirror. She realizes that she must let Oktavian go to young Sophie, for she is approaching middle age which must always make way for youth. No singer has ever captured, quite as Lehmann did, the sadness and the dignity of growing older. Her performance was a masterpiece of operatic characterization.

In 1912 Strauss wrote the incidental music to Molière's comedy, *Le Bourgeois Gentilhomme* (*The Would-be Gentleman*). He intended it to be an evening's entertainment—one that closed with a short opera, *Ariadne auf Naxos*. The play and opera combination was not a success, and Strauss revised it. The second version of *Ariadne* is the one we hear today.

Die Frau ohne Schatten (*The Woman Without a Shadow*) was given in 1919. It is a mystic, exotic allegory that rivals *The Magic Flute* for plot complications. Until recently it has never been a great popular success, and most critics have called it overblown. But when the Metropolitan Opera presented it (1966) in its new home in Lincoln Center, with breathtaking settings and a cast of international stars, it was hailed as a masterpiece!

Intermezzo (1924) and *Die Ägyptische Helena* (*The Egyptian Helen*) (1928) were greeted with cool response from audiences and critics. Perhaps Strauss had not written himself out, as authorities would have us believe, but was only ahead of his time. *Helen* was given a performance by Thomas Scherman and the Little Orchestra Society in 1967 that made an applauding New York audience realize what it had been missing. Ingrid Bjoner was the lovely Helen of Troy, and the brilliant American soprano Elisabeth Carron was the mysterious Aithra.

Strauss was seventy years old when he completed *Arabella* in 1933—a time when Adolf Hitler had set upon a plan that would lead to world-wide destruction.

Strauss's operas of this period, *Die Schweigsame Frau* (*The Silent Woman*) (1935), *Friedenstag* (*The Day of Peace*) (1938), *Daphne* (1938), and *Capriccio* (1939), add to the confusing controversy that surrounded him then and does to this day.

Joseph Goebbels, Hitler's propaganda minister, appointed Strauss to an important position. Strauss accepted and then resigned a few weeks after the premiere of *The Silent Woman*. Had the use of a libretto written by the Jewish Stefan Zweig made the Aryan government angry with him? Or was the aged Strauss taking a stand at last?

It is obvious that all of his last operas suffered in comparison to his truly great works—not from lack of musical invention or perennial youthful imagination, but from poor librettos. His desire to protect the only Strauss he knew—the musical Strauss—is a part of this, too. He felt that he had been betrayed at every turn. During the war years, and after, he found himself part of a German time that did not believe in the eternity of all mankind. He was an old man, and he was surrounded by the immorality of the German nation. He tried to escape to the days of his youth. Attempting to regain some of his love of beauty and laughter, he fell back onto musical trickery.

He died in Garmisch in 1949. The Bavarian town is not far from Munich, where, at seven, he heard his first opera, *Der Freischütz.*

He had become, and is now, the very special love of Munich. The magnificent State Opera there has given more than 1,500 performances of his works—with *Der Rosenkavalier* heading the list (more than 400 performances).

He was buried in Munich's Ostfried cemetery to the sounds of his own *Rosenkavalier's "Hab' mir's gelobt, ihn lieb zu haben* ("I vowed to myself to cherish him in the right way") —one of the most beautiful trios in all opera.

The man who had shown the world—and future composers —how to write music that could shock as well as bring tears to clear eyes and strong hearts, the composer whose orchestras and singers tore into and sang their way to the very limits of physical passion and beauty was laid to rest with the soaring, lyric proof that great beauty is eternal. It cannot die.

CHAPTER TWELVE

La belle France

A review of French nineteenth-century operas reminds one of a lingering visit to an elegant art gallery whose walls are lined with magnificently framed portraits of beautiful women. As we stand before lifelike paintings of the legendary ladies of music history—*Manon, Thaïs, Mélisande, Louise, Mignon, Juliette, Dalila,* and *Carmen*—we realize that the composers of this period were concerned more with the glorification of romantic women than they were with the realities of the times they were living in. No matter. Their fascinating creations live on in opera houses everywhere, proving that even as we head for the twenty-first century, woman is eternal.

Jules Massenet, who was born in 1842, was the son of an ironworker. His mother was a talented pianist and her son's first teacher. At eleven Massenet entered the Paris Conservatory and later studied composition with Ambroise Thomas (1811–1896), the director of the school. Thomas is remembered as the composer of *Mignon* (1866), a charming opera that has had more than two thousand performances at the Opéra-Comique.

During his school days, Jules played the drums several nights a week in a theater orchestra to supplement his nonexistent allowance. In 1863 he won the coveted *Prix de Rome,* a prize that gave him the opportunity to study at the famous Medici Villa. In Rome he met the great Franz Liszt and also the woman who was to be his wife, Mlle Saint-Marie.

His first successful opera was *Le Roi de Lahore* (*The King of Lahore*) (1877). But his great triumphs were to be those operas whose librettos dealt with the delicately perfumed lives of young ladies whose reputations were as fabulous as their beauty.

In 1881, his *Hérodiade* was produced in Brussels. The heroine was Salomé—but a Salome who was a far cry from the demon we discussed in the last chapter. The superb Emma Calvé made her very popular. Lina Cavalieri, an extraordinary beauty of the early 1900s, helped too. Mary Garden wrote about Cavalieri (with all the candor of an archrival): "She was radiant, full of diamonds and beauty. But her singing was awful!"

Manon appeared in 1884 and is accepted as Massenet's masterpiece. Abbé Prévost's story of a convent girl who becomes the toast of Paris gave Massenet's gifts for writing sensuous, romantic, singable music full expression. In the first act, Manon comments: "How pleasant it must be to amuse oneself for one's whole life." With this provocative line she tells us much of her character and also explains many of Massenet's heroines.

Of course, Manon meets the fate allotted to all bad girls of her time, and she dies in the gray mists that surround Le Havre.

Manon has fascinated many sopranos since her first appearance. Some of the best interpreters of this romantic role have been Bidu Sayão, Grace Moore, Jarmila Novotna, and Beverly Sills.

Massenet wrote thirty popular operas during his lifetime, and he saw them all produced. Of these, only *Manon, Thaïs* (1894), *Le jongleur de Notre Dame* (*The Juggler of Notre Dame*) (1902) and *Werther* (1892), are performed with any regularity.

In *Thaïs,* one of Mary Garden's special roles, Massenet, who was always one to recognize what appealed to the public, reversed his good-bad girl theme. *Thaïs,* successfully "bad" in the first act, dies redeemed—in a convent.

Despite modern criticism, *Thaïs* is a colorful drama, and it has much beautiful music. Its quiet intermezzo, the meditation, has been played to death by orchestras, violinists, and cocktail-lounge pianists, but its charm is still apparent.

Camille Saint-Saëns (1835–1921) should be mentioned for his *Samson et Dalila,* which was first performed in 1877. It is actually an oratorio with dramatic action. It is memorable for its seductive aria, *"Mon coeur S'ouvre à ta voix"* ("My Heart at thy Sweet Voice"), which has been sung unforgettably and agonizingly by almost every contralto or mezzo in the world since its first performance. The opera is based on the biblical story of the mighty Samson who loses his strength when his hair is cut by the temptress Delilah.

Robert Merrill, baritone of the Met, tells an amusing incident about the opera that conveys some of the eccentricities of singers—and the mishaps that can occur in opera performances.

He relates in his amusing book, *Once More from the Beginning,* a story about tenor Kurt Baum, who was high-C crazy and who sang the role of Samson. In the last act, Samson prays for his strength to be returned and his prayers are answered. With the help of fall-away scenery (and stagehands) the vigorous Samson pushes the columns of the temple apart, and all the evil Philistines are destroyed. Mr. Baum was singing away, anticipating his final high C, when the stagehands mistook a cue and brought the scenery down on the whole cast before the called-for time. Mr. Baum was not daunted—he pulled himself up from the rubble and hit his high C!

One of the most popular French operas is *Faust* by Charles Gounod. It is, to date, probably the most performed opera in France. It has been presented all over the world, it has been the gala opening night at the Met, and it was given a new production there (1965) with stage direction by the great French actor Jean-Louis Barrault. At that occasion, the Walpurgis Night ballet sequence, which was not a part of the original *Faust* (1859), caused almost as much furor as *Salome* did fifty years ago.

Faust endures and is performed in many, many languages for the simple reason that it is full of melody and spectacle. And it tells Goethe's story of human frailty with simplicity and craftsmanship.

The most famous arias from *Faust* are Marguerite's "*Air des bijoux*" (Jewel song), Méphistophéles' *Le Veau d'or* (Song of the golden calf), Valentine's "*Avant de quitter ces lieux*" ("Even the Bravest Heart May Swell"), and, of course, Faust's impassioned "*Salut! demeure chaste et pure*" ("Hail, So Pure and Chaste") with its ringing high C.

Gounod also wrote *Roméo et Juliette,* whose sparkling waltz song for its young leading lady was about the only part of it that appealed to American audiences—except in rare productions that could boast the unusual talents of Bidu Sayão and Richard Crooks. Or, when in 1968, audiences discovered that they could easily identify with this opera version of Shakespeare's play when the star-crossed lovers were sung by youthful and physically attractive singers like Franco Corelli and Mirella Freni.

Gounod was a composer of taste and refinement, and his operas are, without exception, truly French.

French operas were regular and anticipated operatic fare in the United States during the early twentieth century, chiefly because there were artists who were capable of performing them with elegance and the pointed sound so necessary to the language. As the performing style degenerated and singers who had no empathy for the language itself tried, unfortunately, to achieve the French sound by singing through their noses, these beautiful lyric works began to disappear. They did not, however, before audiences had responded to Debussy's *Pelléas et Mélisande.* To this day *Pelléas* is the subject of much controversy. Ernest Newman, the revered music critic of the London Sunday *Times* and author of the monumental four-volume biography *The Life of Richard Wagner,* spoke of it as "a sort of glorified musical mule without pride of ancestry or hope of posterity." Pitts Sanborn, the well-informed music critic and musicologist of the '30s, called it "unique and isolated in the history of opera." Mary Garden recalled that "every critic in Paris denounced *Pelléas.* They said it had no spine and no rhythm. But the public, *that* was different. After five performances, the Opéra-Comique became a cathedral!"

In all fairness to its admirers and its dissenters, *Pelléas* is very special and very different. One does not encounter a single aria or chorus in the opera. It is a shadowy, misty, lost-world painting brought to musical life by Claude Debussy's hypnotic ability to weave music and words together into a perfect opera. His orchestra whispers and sighs—never raises its voice hysterically. His music follows the words of Maeterlinck's play with loving affection and pays attention to his every vowel and consonant.

At the premiere of *Pelléas and Mélisande* in 1902, sensitive listeners and some sensitive critics realized that they had heard the French language and the text of an opera—with all its nuance and subtlety—in a new format. The vague story had been meticulously enhanced by a composer who could suggest and paint with sound.

Debussy defended his masterpiece by saying: "I have tried to obey a law of beauty which appears to be singularly ignored in dealing with dramatic music. The characters in this drama endeavor to sing like real persons rather than in the traditional manner of operas constructed on some arbitrary and antiquated pattern. I do not pretend to have discovered anything in *Pelléas*. But I have tried to mark a path which others may follow and make broader with their own discoveries, in such a way, perhaps, as to liberate dramatic music from the heavy yoke it has been wearing for so long."

That he succeeded, there is little doubt. The authoritative critic Virgil Thomson paid tribute to Debussy by saying:

"Modern music, the full flower of it, the achievement rather than the hope, stems from Debussy. Everybody who wrote before him is just an ancestor and belongs to another time. Debussy belongs to ours . . . certainly modern music, all of it, could be rebuilt from the works of Debussy."

Claude Achille Debussy (1862–1918) was the adventuresome creator of impressionism in music. He, like many of the painters, poets, and dramatists of the time, was concerned with expressing personal passion and sensitivity. Debussy went a step farther by composing music that depicted passion and sensitivity when they became involved with unusual situations and unexpected moods. He refused to explain musically or to compose graphic, realistically detailed, note-by-note descriptions. His music suggested. He wanted his musical images to conjure up emotions in the hearer—emotions that would carry on beyond mere recognition of a place or situation. His orchestra and voices were his means of expressing the timelessness of feelings and memory—recaptured or lost. Mélisande is discovered in a forest—not a particular forest, but every mysterious forest of one's dreams. We are not even sure *who* Mélisande is. When she dies, even she is not certain why she has been involved in the gray, unanswerable sequence of events that have made up her life. But Debussy's musical brush paints an illusive, and yet real, canvas of suggested things. He makes us feel the necessity of dreaming and exploring the unknown. Probably the most famous Mélisande of all time was Mary Garden. She sang the first performance of the opera, much against the wishes of Maurice Maeterlinck, who had written the play. Garden was coached by the composer, and her interpretation has become legend. French audiences may have smiled at her American accent, but they were quick to realize that the amazing singing actress was a unique and impressive impressionist.

Garden had made her debut at the Opéra-Comique in 1900 under circumstances as volatile as her personality. On Friday, April 13, she replaced the indisposed soprano who was singing the title role of Charpentier's *Louise* and became an immediate star. She sang more than one hundred performances of *Louise* throughout her colorful career.

Wallace Fowlie wrote in *Pantomime:*

"She *was* the work symbolically, ritualistically, standing before us all in her always imminent stage of vulnerability. She acted and sang as if she were at all times on the verge of being sacrificed, but she was delirious with the idea as if it achieved her and translated her into ultimate reality. Mary Garden caused me to feel the religious aspect of the theater long before I read in books that the origins of the theater were religious practices. . . . I watched *Louise* as if it were a mystery play. When she sang *Depuis le jour* to Julien I marveled how the intensity of love increased the solitude of the lover. When Mary Garden sang the words: *Ah, I am happy! So very happy!* she was already announcing her ultimate flight, the rushing out into the dark and the dispersal of all the emotion which she kept contained within her as she sang."

Louise is Gustave Charpentier's (1860–1956) major claim to fame. It is naturalistic opera, and his score sings with the colorful sounds of Paris. Its story, about a young seamstress who runs away to Montmartre with her poet-lover, was considered very daring in 1900. Andrew Carnegie would not go to hear it

—even with the great Garden—because he did not believe in free love. That was hardly the subject of the opera. Charpentier was really writing an opera about Paris. The city and her people intrigued him and obsessed him all of his life. He was also writing about the need for young people to express themselves in the terms of their time.

Louise's most famous aria is *"Depuis le jour"* ("Ever Since the Day"). Now that American audiences have been deprived of the gifted soprano, Grace Moore, the opera has not been able to hold its own in the repertory of our opera houses.

That can never be said of another beautiful operatic heroine —*Carmen*. Musical history has something in common with political history—some of its legends hold no truth. *Carmen's* first performance is an example. There are those who persist in having us believe that its "failure" was the cause of its composer's early death. But the learned Maurice Tassart, a French writer and authority on Bizet, assures us that *Carmen* had eleven performances a month during the three-month period following its premiere in 1875. Bizet died, at thirty-six, on the evening of the gypsy's thirty-third appearance, not from a broken heart but from a ruptured artery.

Georges Bizet (1838–1875) was born in Paris. His father was a singing teacher and his mother an accomplished pianist. Both furthered his obvious and precocious musical gifts. There was never any doubt that he was going to be a celebrated composer. His virtuoso piano performances brought him to the attention of Liszt, Berlioz, and Saint-Saëns, and at nineteen he had won the Prix de Rome.

Oddly enough, his abundant gifts—his musicality, his craftsmanship, and his originality—never interfered with his being a likable and easy-to-get-along-with man.

His first opera, *Les Pecheurs de Perles* (*The Pearl Fishers*) (1863), *La Jolie Fille de Perth* (*The Fair Maid of Perth*) (1876), and *Djamileh* (1872), were not greeted with unstinting praise or overly warm public reaction. However, after the success of *Carmen,* they did return to the repertory of French opera houses and they still enjoy performances in that country.

Carmen's libretto was prepared by Meilhac and Halévy. In comparison to the original gypsy creation of Prosper Mérimée, the opera's fiery protagonist has been sketched in pastel colors. But, modified as she was for Bizet's version, the "wicked" girl still managed to horrify some of the Parisian public.

Mérimée's *Carmen,* published thirty years before the gypsy danced across the stage of the Opéra-Comique, was an earthy novella about a tantalizing thief who was also involved in several murders.

Not daring, or wanting to go too far with the decorous French, Bizet and his librettists cut away the more scandalous aspects of the lurid gypsy's personality. They also added the character of Micaëla, a pallid village girl. Her purity and love for the hero, Don José, were intended tonal contrasts to the more devilish freedom-loving Carmen. They also gave Micaëla a touching song to sing in Act III, *"Je dis, que rien ne m'épouvante"* ("I can say that nothing frightens me"), that can stop the show.

Carmen's creators obviously knew what they were doing, because the early opera audiences took the sweet Micaëla to their hearts. Now she is looked upon as being close to simple-minded, and contemporary operagoers look forward to an "all-out" *Carmen* performance that more closely resembles the original Mérimée conception.

Carmen—with its spoken recitatives—marked up more than 2,900 Paris performances at the Opéra-Comique before it was transferred (with sung recitatives—by Ernest Guiraud) to the grand Théâtre de l'Opéra. There is generous proof that *Carmen* is probably the most performed opera in the world. And we need only mention that one of the most famous of American *Carmens*, Coe Glade, sang some 3,000 performances of this remarkable opera during her career!

Hearing *Carmen* could convince us that Bizet had lived in the mountains of Spain and had walked the streets of Seville. He had not. All of *Carmen*'s Spanish sunlight and haunting rhythms are from the mind's eye and ear of a man who never visited that part of the world.

The score abounds with famous songs. In the first act, Carmen sings her "Habanera," a catchy, alluring Cuban dance rhythm, and then, to convince Don José that he must allow her to escape, she lures him with a "Seguidilla." The toreador, Escamillo, sings his famous "Toreador Song" in Act II. It has become one of the most popular baritone arias in all opera.

Carmen's gripping song, when she reads the forecast of death from her pack of tarot cards (Act III), is another memorable part of the opera—particularly, if one succumbs to the possibility that the very first interpreter of the role, Célestine Galli-Marié, was turning the card of death up—onstage—as Bizet died. The years have only increased *Carmen*'s popularity, and she is the sought-after challenge of every important and unimportant mezzo-soprano or contralto. At one time operagoers thought of Carmen and Emma Calvé as being one. Today, the list of superlative interpreters of the role is legion. Glade, Risë Stevens, Regina Resnik, Constance Shacklock, Nell Rankin, Jean Madeira, and, on a supercharged recording, the versatile Callas.

When asked if she thought Carmen is a bad woman, Maria Callas replied: "Of course not, she's a *gypsy*. She thinks that her destiny is preordained, that nothing can change it. Consequently, she feels, why not act according to the impulses of the moment? Carmen's morality is never to pretend what she does not really feel. She is not calculating, but she *is* ruthless."

All the beautiful heroines of French opera linger with us and sing to us with their many voices—frail, mysterious, dynamic, love-struck. But Carmen's bronze voice and the wicked fire in her eyes seem to say that the tarot cards told her, many years ago, what we all know today: *Carmen* was destined to be the most popular of them all.

$\mathcal{U}$im, $\mathcal{U}$igor, and $\mathcal{U}$iolence Equal $\mathcal{U}$erismo

Red-blooded Italian opera lovers became bored with the subtle escapades of the musical heroines we have just discussed. Romain Rolland, one of the great music scholars of the twentieth century, wrote in *Essays on Music:* "The Italian refers everything to himself. It is neither the action nor the characters that interest him. It is the passions; he embraces them all; he experiences them all in his own person. Hence the frenzied exaltation into which opera throws him at certain moments. In no other country has the love of opera this passionate quality because no other nation displays this personal egotistical character. The Italian does not go to the opera house to see the heroes of opera but to see himself, to hear himself, to caress and inflame his passions."

Thus the languorous women and their subtle perfumes were thrust aside in favor of operas with the smell of the earth and realism. The larger-than-life "realism" of murder, hatred, violence, and passion.

Taut, melodramatic operas—some of them of only one-act duration—lunged through Italy and Europe leaving their musical imprint of blood and horror on many composers of that time, as well as composers to come.

During the reign of operatic violence, composers vied with one another in setting bloodcurdling librettos to descriptive, and often lurid, music. Their aims were direct, to say the least. They let the leading singers declaim dramatically and sing out with burning intensity. And their orchestras accompanied them with lush, theatrical harmonic effects. Occasionally a short chorus piece or an instrumental interlude would be cleverly placed in the opera to give the audience a chance to catch its breath and prepare to be ripped apart again.

One of the earliest *verismo* operas was Amilcare Ponchielli's (1834–1886) *La Gioconda* (*The Joyous One*). It can be translated as *The Joyful Girl,* if you like. The fact that the title is the name of its leading character—an Italian street singer—adds a little *verismo* irony to the whole affair. That the girl could ever be joyful, particularly considering what she is confronted with during the four acts of the opera, is highly unlikely.

The opera is based on a play by Victor Hugo, and it is set in Venice during the Inquisition. Gioconda's mother is blind, and Gioconda is in love with Enzo—who is in love with Laura. These basics give one just a vague idea of the girl's initial problems. In addition, she is being pursued by the villainous Barnaba, a powerful leader of the Inquisition. To lighten the melodrama and the awareness of terrible tortures that are taking place behind the ornate, golden doors of the palaces, we are allowed the pleasures of a famous ballet—"The Dance of the Hours."

Then we plunge on into the death of Gioconda's mother and the singer's suicide. All of these incredulous goings-on are smiled at by many. Indeed, much of the music is second-rate, but a quartet of magnificent singers can make an exciting evening out of *La Gioconda.*

The opera was given its first performance in Milan in 1876. Three of its famous arias are worth mentioning: Cieca's "*Voce di Donna*" (Is It the Voice of a Woman or an Angel?"), Enzo's rapturous, "*Cielo e mar*" ("O, Sky and Sea!"), and Gioconda's spine-chilling decision to kill herself rather than give in to Barnaba, "*Suicidio!*" ("Suicide! Now that is All that Is Left for Me"). This a real *verismo* singer's opera. One is made aware of it when it is in the hands—and voices—of great stars like Zinka Milanov, the late Leonard Warren, Callas, and the Italian mezzo, Fiorenza Cossotto.

In 1890, the Costanzi Theater in Rome was the scene of an electrifying one-act shocker that rocked the opera world. It was called *Cavalleria Rusticana* (*Rustic Chivalry*). Its unrelenting story and music forge ahead with only one lyrical interruption—a lovely intermezzo that celebrates the glory of Easter. The locale is Sicily, which everyone knows is inhabited by strong-willed people who have no intention of taking second place to volcanoes.

Pietro Mascagni (1863–1945), composer of *Cavalleria Rusticana,* was the son of a baker. The elder Mascagni did everything in his power to discourage the boy's musical ambitions, and it was due only to the forthright understanding of an uncle that the youngster's composing career was not ruined. He subsequently led a rough, poverty-ridden life traveling all over Italy as a conductor. But *Cavalleria*'s first performance—when he was twenty-seven—made him an overnight sensation. The dramatic aria for the heroine, Santuzza, "*Voi lo sapete, o*

mamma" ("You Know It Well, Mother"), is one of the melodic highlights of the opera, which is a theatrical block-buster
that runs the gamut of betrayal, excommunication, hatred, infidelity, and murder—all blessedly accompanied by stunning,
singable melodies that remain in the listener's mind long after
the curtain has come down.

Emma Eames was the first Metropolitan Santuzza (1891).
Some of the other memorable interpreters of this great dra-
matic-soprano role have been Maria Jeritza, Rosa Ponselle,
Maria Caniglia, Dusolina Giannini, Eva Turner, and Giulietta
Simionato.

Mascagni tried desperately to duplicate the success of his
first triumph, but he failed. His *Iris* and *L'Amico Fritz* never
appealed to his shock-hungry public even when he relegated
the heroine of *Iris* to a seamy death in a sewer!

Another sizzler, one that is usually paired with *Cavalleria
Rusticana,* is *I Pagliacci (The Clowns)*, by Ruggiero Leoncavallo (1858–1919). Leoncavallo's *I Pagliacci* was premiered in
Milan, 1892. The composer wrote his own libretto for this
brooding Calabrian play within a play that covers one eventful
day in the lives of a troupe of traveling actors.

From the moment Tonio appears and sings the prologue we
are compelled to listen and become aware of the work of a
master of *verismo*. Leoncavallo, like Mascagni, made audiences
cognizant that the tragedies of the common man could be just
as terrible and powerful as those of the gods.

After Nedda's lilting *"Ballatella"* (Bird song) and the haunting love duet we hear one of the most enduringly popular
tenor songs ever written—Canio's *"Vesti la giubba"* ("Put on
the Mask"). Canio was one of Enrico Caruso's greatest roles.

His performances of this opera made his name a household word throughout the world. His glory remains undimmed, and, as if by some miracle, his recordings of this aria, despite the technical limitations of the times, still disclose the burnished beauty of his unparalleled voice. When Canio sobs: *"La commedia è finita"* ("The comedy is over") and collapses on the steps of the little stage, we know we have been a part of real *verismo* tragedy.

Leoncavallo, like Mascagni, failed to achieve again anything like the overwhelming success of his first opera. *Zaza* impressed some in 1900, but it is almost forgotten. *Zaza* also attracted some attention when interpreted by the star of stars, Geraldine Farrar. There are those who suspect that it was due to Miss Farrar's discreet striptease during the performance— not the heroine's musical or dramatic qualifications.

Umberto Giordano was another *verismo* composer whose claim to fame rests on one opera. His *Andrea Chénier* (1896) is a flamboyant and melodramatic opera about the Revolutionary poet, André de Chénier. Today it is old hat and remains in the repertory only to be drawn out as a vehicle for a reigning tenor or soprano who can make memorable the last scene —when Chénier and Maddalena go to face death on the guillotine.

As was to be expected, *verismo* was due for a quick death. Its themes, both in terms of music and libretto, were so desperate and so determined to burn that the flames, no matter how colorful, were destined to extinguish themselves quickly.

Giacomo Puccini (1858–1924) was born into music. His ancestors had been musicians for more than one hundred and fifty years. One of his teachers was Ponchielli, and by the time he was twenty-five, Puccini had seen his first opera, *Le Villi,* produced at La Scala.

Manon Lescaut (1893) established him as a composer worthy of attention.

His third opera, *La Bohème* (1896) was the first of a dazzling series of superb operas that made Puccini—along with Verdi—one of the most adored and respected composers in operatic history. Puccini was, in addition to being a supreme writer of melody, a showman whose mind was brilliantly attuned to the craft of the theater. He was demanding with his librettists and himself, and his collaboration with Giacosa and Illica (two fine writers) continued throughout several operas.

La Bohème, with its endearing story of a group of poor, young artists searching for their identity (and for recognition of their talent in the Latin Quarter of Paris), has remained, and rightfully so, one of the most popular operas of all time. Its touching songs were at the top of the charts in the operatic poll of 1896, and they hold their own today.

As a youth, Puccini had known poverty and the burning desire for recognition in Milan. His complete understanding of Murger's characters is touchingly apparent in melodies. All of the four episodes that make up *La Bohème* have memorable music. Act I, after Mimi and Rodolfo meet for the first time in the poet's dingy attic room, introduces the tenor's lovely *"Che gelida manina"* ("Your Little Hand Is Frozen"). It is followed by the soprano's touching *"Mi chiamano Mimi"* ("They Call me Mimi, but my name is Lucia"). In this aria she narrates, with heartbreaking candor, how she embroiders the flowers of her fantasy world onto dresses and silken materials to earn a meager living. The scene closes with winter moonlight flooding the room and the couple swearing enduring love.

The music of *La Bohème* immediately confirms the Puccini trademarks—sensuous, singing melody, a clever use of dissonance, series of chords, and an unfailing and infallible sense of what constitutes good theater.

Sardou's melodrama, *La Tosca,* which he had written for the great actress Sarah Bernhardt, was the foundation of Puccini's next success. The play, about a famous prima donna, Floria Tosca, and the despised Roman chief of police, Baron Scarpia, became even more famous as an opera.

Scarpia, the villain, and the sequence of events surrounding him, defy one's imagination, but from the moment the curtain goes up—following only three blatant chords from the orchestra—Puccini glamorizes the musty plot and his characters with theatrical, romantic music that never loses its hold.

Tosca's aria, *"Vissi d'arte, vissi d'amore"* ("I Have Lived for Art and for Love") is a moving and lovely prayer that should soften the heart of any chief of police. It doesn't. The beautiful singer has to kill him to escape. Grateful as we may be for his death, we are more appreciative of the bloodcurdling scene that follows. To muted orchestral accompaniment, Tosca removes a crucifix from the wall to place on Scarpia's body. Suddenly there is a hair-raising roll of drums. She drops the crucifix in terror and slowly leaves the room. *Verismo* melodrama at its best!

The last act opens almost immediately with an aria for the tenor, Cavaradossi, *"E lucevan le Stelle"* ("The Stars Were Brightly Shining"). When it is sung by a fine artist, it sparks a reaction equal to a home run by the Mets. Encores are allowed in European opera houses but never at the Metropolitan. The list of notable Toscas would fill a page. The most memorable are: Hariclea Darclée (premiere), Milka Ternina, Maria Jeritza, who started a fad by singing her famous aria lying flat on her tummy, Claudia Muzio, Gina Cigna, Callas, and Marie Collier. The last Callas performances of this opera commanded as much as $100 for a single ticket!

Madame Butterfly (1904) was a disaster. But when the pathetic geisha girl returned the following year, she was a complete triumph. The exotic story of a lovely Japanese girl who is deserted by a callous American naval officer was a natural for Puccini. It shows his fondness for Orientalism, and he used the odd harmonies and rhythmic patterns of the East to fine effect in both *Madame Butterfly* and *Turandot.*

Cio-Cio-San's affirmative and beautiful aria, *"Un bel dì"* ("One Fine Day He Will Come"), still manages to produce many handkerchiefs in opera houses all over the world.

Salomea Krusceniski was the Butterfly of the revised and successful second performance in Brescia, Italy, and Emmy Destinn was the ill-fated heroine at its Covent Garden premiere. In America, during the early part of the century, the role was almost exclusively the property of Geraldine Farrar. But, as the opera continued to increase in popularity, many sopranos brought their distinctive interpretive powers to the role. Among the most telling have been Licia Albanese, Jarmila Novotna, Dorothy Kirsten, and Elisabeth Carron.

La Fanciulla del West (*The Girl of the Golden West*) was produced in New York, 1910. It was a smashing success at the time, but Puccini's version of our wild and turbulent California has diminished in popularity over the years. *Verismo,* American-style or not—audiences have never really taken to this obvious thriller—much less to the scene where the heroine, Minnie, and the sheriff gamble at a game of cards—with her lover's life as the stakes—while drops of blood are dripping from the loft overhead!

La Rondine (*The Swallow*) (1917) is pale and operetta-like in comparison with Puccini's major successes, and it was not until 1918 that the composer found himself back in the affections of his public.

Three one-act operas comprise *Il Trittico*. They are: *Gianni Schicchi, a* boisterous *commedia dell'arte* farce about a wily Italian who turns the tables on a group of greedy Florentines; *Il Tabarro* (*The Cloak*), a grim melodrama of life and infidelity on a seamy barge, and *Suor Angelica* (*Sister Angelica*), a rhapsodically scored piece whose miracle-play aspects are oddly unconvincing. *Il Trittico* was premiered in New York in 1918, and the enterprising New York City Opera Company, Lincoln Center, keeps its bright and amusing verison of it in its adventuresome repertory.

Puccini never completed his last opera, a Chinese fairy tale, *Turandot.* He died in 1924, following an operation for cancer of the throat. Only the closing duet was unfinished, and that was put together by Franco Alfano—using themes and melodies from the rest of the opera. Arturo Toscanini was the conductor for *Turandot's* first La Scala performance. When he and the orchestra reached the last notes from Puccini's pen, he turned to the audience and said, "At this point the Maestro laid down his pen."

Turandot is a colorful spectacle and an enduring testament to the Italian master's immortal gift for melody. The opera is also the framework for one of the most taxing and spectacular soprano roles in opera history—the evil Princess Turandot.

No soprano has ever diminished Eva Turner's shining performances in this role, but any history must pay tribute to Rosa Raisa (premiere), Anne Roselle, Leonie Rysanek, and the gleaming Birgit Nilsson as superlative interpreters of the Princess of Ice.

With Puccini, the fires of *verismo* were refined and enhanced by immortal romantic melodies. Italo Montemezzi (1875–1952) discarded anything that smacked of shock and wrote a beautiful, lyric tragedy, *L'amore dei tre re* (*The Love of Three Kings*).

Montemezzi's score pays subtle but honest homage to the music of Wagner and Debussy. It also favors the chromaticism of Puccini. But most important are Montemezzi's natural sense of melody and his distinctive, noble style. *The Love of Three Kings* was premiered in 1913. That Donald Jay Grout, Given Foundation professor of musicology at Cornell University, calls it "one of the best Italian tragic operas since Verdi's *Otello*" is formidable recommendation. Its haunting music should be revived more often, if only to remind us that romantic Italian opera survived the smoldering ashes of *verismo*, burned again in the thrilling melodic theatrics of Puccini, and lives today in hundreds of opera houses.

CHAPTER FOURTEEN

The Russians, the Bohemians, and Chaliapin

Credit should be given to Catherine the Great for introducing opera to the aristocracy of Russia. It is not unusual that a monarch, whose life resembled a *verismo* libretto, should be the one to invite cosmopolitan composers to come to St. Petersburg and assist her in making it a music center to rival Paris and London. These beginnings were limited, of course, to the nobility, but they were beginnings that led to a dramatic nationalistic movement in that part of the world.

German-born Catherine, in addition to being notorious, had brains and imagination. She was also wise enough to know that a part of Russia would live through Russian music. During her thirty-four-year reign, not only imported operas were performed, but also theater pieces with Russian librettos came to light. The most important composer of this period was Evstigney Fomin. During 1786 and 1800 he gave St. Petersburg audiences several operas, the most notable being *The Coachman* (1787) with an authentic Russian score that utilized genuine folk material.

Oddly enough, an Italian, Catterino Cavos, who was invited

to Russia in 1799—and became so popular he stayed for the rest of his life—also made important advances for Russian opera. His *Ivan Susanin* (1815) was for many years the much admired example of what nationalistic opera should be.

Mikhail Glinka (1804–1857) used the same story line for his opera dealing with the life of Ivan Susanin. Originally performed under the title of *A Life for the Czar,* it is heard in Russia and Europe today as simply, *Ivan Susanin.* Although its music is obviously eclectic and modern hearers are inclined to hear much of Italy and France—as well as Russia—in its score, the opera's supercharged choruses so excited the public that one of them practically became a national hymn. Glinka's second opera, *Russlan and Ludmilla* (1842), though never as popular as *Ivan,* really established Russian music for Russians.

He also split the camp of Russian composers in two. On the left were Tchaikovsky, Anton Rubinstein, and Nikolai Rubinstein. On the right were Balakirev, Borodin, Mussorgsky, Rimsky-Korsakov, and Cui—a formidable group that became known as the Russian Five.

The group of three was headed by Piotr Ilyich Tchaikovsky (1840–1893). His operas, concerned though they were with Russian themes and Russian locales, were personal works. They were moody, filled with melancholia and romance, and showed ample evidence of the composer's admiration for the music of Italy and France.

Tchaikovsky was a far cry from the child-genius type of composer that frequents the pages of this history. The thought never occurred to him or his parents that he should concentrate on music, much less dedicate his life to it. By the time he was nineteen, he was working as a government clerk. At twenty, he suddenly reached the conclusion that he was not doing what he wanted to do and that, perhaps, he might have the talent for a musical career. It appears that whether he reached a decision or not, his efforts were not successfully concentrated enough to allow him to discard his obvious dilettante life in favor of serious work. Major changes began to take place when Nikolai Rubinstein offered him a post at the Conservatory in Moscow. Rubinstein also encouraged Tchaikovsky's composing and saw to it that his compositions were heard. His Overture-Fantasy, *Romeo and Juliet,* was acclaimed in Moscow, and he settled down to serious work—and to a life as melancholy as his music.

Of some nine operas, *Eugene Onegin* (1879) and *The Queen of Spades* (1890) are the most notable. Both are based on stories by the great Russian poet Pushkin.

Eugene Onegin was not successful at its first performance. The composer accredits the poor response to bad performances by the singers. The opera was revived in 1884, and evidently the singers interpreted the music with some spirit because *Onegin* became more popular than the perennial box-office favorite, *A Life for the Czar.* The opera is one of Tchaikovsky's happiest scores, and he has surrounded his heroine, Tatiana, and the hero, Onegin, with romantic melodies and beautiful orchestrations.

The most famous scene from *Onegin* involves Tatiana. It contains some of Tchaikovsky's most haunting vocal music and captures completely Tatania's adoration of Onegin and its accompanying frustrations.

Eugene Onegin's first American performance was at the Metopolitan Opera in 1920. Tchaikovsky had died of cholera seven years before.

The Queen of Spades is a melodrama dealing with the fate of a compulsive gambler, a heroine who throws herself in the river, a mysterious countess, and a ghost for good measure. This opera has never been popular in America, but the colorful role of the ancient Countess—interpreted by a great singing-actress—is a tour de force of opera.

Marianna Radev, who has interpreted the role of the Countess many times in Europe, has written very illuminatingly about the opera and this role: "It offers us a panorama of the social life of the aristocracy at the beginning of the nineteenth century. At the same time it is a 'horror tale' par excellence. As in Onegin, the heterogeneous dramatic action and, above all, the variety of the melodrama, prove an ideal framework for the music of Tchaikovsky. His artistic approach, which reminds me of that of Tennessee Williams in the contemporary theater, is not so much concerned with shaping some *new* aesthetic concepts and values as using established ones. This approach (the result of what may be called a feminine type of creativity) is realized above all in the depiction of the atmosphere and the characters, thus giving almost unlimited opportunities for individual interpretations on the stage.

"A typical example of Tchaikovsky's use of established concepts—and to great effect—is his lifting of Grétry's lovely song from his opera *Richard Coeur de Lion*. As the old Countess sings it in the scene before her death, it becomes the ghostly reminder of the fleetingness of everything in the world."

We can cut the group of Five down to three by explaining

that Balakirev did not write any operas and César Cui did nothing to advance the national opera of Russia.

Alexander Borodin (1833–1887) was a doctor. He, like all the Five except Rimsky-Korsakov, was an amateur—in the best sense of the word. His *Prince Igor* (1890) is more of an example of inspiration than a monument of great music. Its thundering, primitive music is exciting, but *Prince Igor* is remembered today for its noisy, warlike, leaping Polovetzian Dances and the fact that it introduced the unforgettable Feodor Chaliapin to Western audiences.

The basso was born in 1873, and his unique musical and theatrical gifts have never been duplicated. Everything about him was stunningly primitive and larger than life. His luckless imitators were to find out that his completely original conceptions could not be copied. They persisted anyway. Chaliapin was a singing actor who was bored with *bel canto*. Marvelous voices, for themselves alone, did not interest him. He was obsessed with finding the truth of a character through the words *and* the music. The fact that Chaliapin was born of peasants who could not afford to provide their son with even the rudiments of an education did nothing to deter the boy. At seventeen he had trained himself enough to join a small opera company, and at twenty-three he was a member of the famous Private Opera in Moscow.

The magnitude of Chaliapin's operatic gifts and his personality combined with the grandoise theatrical settings of the Maryinsky Theater opened the eyes and the ears of Paris and London. Chaliapin and everything Russian became the rage of the West. He could mesmerize an audience to such a point that on the occasion of a public rehearsal of *Boris Godunov* in

Paris in 1908, the spectators stood up in order that they could *see* what Chaliapin was staring at in a darkened corner of the stage. There was nothing there, but his psychological involvement in the role had convinced them there was! Of all his roles, *Boris* was his greatest.

The composer of *Boris Godunov,* Modest Mussorgsky (1839–1881) was the child of Russian landowners who lost their modest fortune when the serfs were freed—just prior to the abolishment of slavery in the United States. Living with peasants, on what remained of the family property, brought him into close contact with real life. He attempted a romantic opera using a text by Flaubert that did nothing more than prove to him that his way was destined to be with the people —not the privileged few.

Pushkin's *Boris Godunov,* a drama whose leading character was a historically real, half-crazy czar who controlled Russia for eight years, offered Mussorgsky the perfect story for an opera—an opera that would sing and weep for the Russian people, and it could also inspire them to recognize their potential glory. In *Boris,* Mussorgsky used a type of song-speech that is particularly natural and effective. Also, his melodies are used to interpret the text with a directness that was unique for his time. This direct force remains today one of its most important attributes.

The spectacle of the Coronation scene, with the joyous and deafening tolling of bells, the Farewell of Boris, and the final scene—set in an ominous forest with the character of the Fool lamenting the fate of Russia—contain powerful and original music. *Boris Godunov* was first performed at the Maryinsky, St. Petersburg, in 1874.

It is interesting that the greatest Boris of them all, Chalia-pin, who believed himself *of* the people, found the Commu-nists as hard to take as he had the Czarists. He died in exile, reminiscing perhaps on the words of Pushkin's Fool: "weep, weep, you people. Weep, Russia, for soon the gloom will fall."

At forty-two, Modest Mussorgsky was dead. Dead of over-work, alcohol, drugs, and prolonged sicknesses. Fortunately he had finished the first draft of *Khovantchina* and some of the scenes for *The Fair at Sorochinsk*. Both were eventually com-pleted by other composers and subsequently were heard throughout the world.

Nikolai Rimsky-Korsakov (1844–1908) wrote operas that were the exact opposite of Mussorgsky's. For Rimsky the rea-son for opera was the music. Fantastic, exotic fairy tales which allowed him to use many folk songs, rather than serious, realis-tic plots, attracted him. Nikolai was born into an aristocratic family, and he entered the Naval College in St. Petersburg at the age of twelve. At seventeen he met Balakirev who was probably the major influence that turned Nikolai to thinking of becoming a serious musician. Any plans he may have had at the time were delayed, for he was sent on a three-year cruise. His *Symphony No. 1* was composed during those years and was performed in St. Petersburg in 1865. Its success was a de-termining factor in Nikolai's decision to stay in that city and pursue a career in music.

In 1871, following the great acclaim for his opera *The Maid of Pskov,* he was appointed a professor at the Conservatory in St. Petersburg. Orchestration was one of his subjects, and rightfully so, for the brilliant young man was eventually to write a book on orchestration that remains a Bible for all arrangers and orchestrators.

The Snow Maiden (*Snegurochka*), a fairy tale with touches of symbolism, made its first appearance in 1882.

Sadko, which is considered Rimsky-Korsakov's masterpiece, was first performed in 1898. It is a fantasy complete with myriad opportunities for spectacle and the combination of Oriental colors with Russian themes. Rimsky had a unique gift for writing perfect music for fantastic situations and unreal creatures. Only he could have written the delightful atmospheric descriptions of Sadko's descent into the aquamarine depths of the ocean to meet the King of the Sea, or, for that matter, the ever popular symphonic poem *Scheherazade.*

The Legend of the Invisible City of Kitezh (1907) and *Le Coq d'or* (*The Golden Cockerel*) (not performed until 1909) were his last operas. When he died at the age of sixty-four, of a heart attack, Rimsky-Korsakov had established himself as an important Russian composer and also as one of the greatest geniuses the orchestra will ever know.

He had also encouraged and taught many future great composers, Igor Stravinsky among them. He had carried Russian music to new and popular heights, and he had never wavered from his belief in the dignity of man. Considering the fact that in 1905 he was dismissed from the St. Petersburg Conservatory because he complained of the overbearing police supervision that the school subjected its students to, he was indeed a man ahead of his time—morally and musically.

Bohemia and the Bohemians should not be confused with the characters of Puccini's famous opera. The nation that we know today as Czechoslovakia was once called Bohemia. The dense Bohemian forest separates the fertile Czech hills from Germany. Czechoslovakia's famous river, the Moldau, is now a part of musical history because of the nostalgic flowing musical tone poem by Bedřich Smetana (1824–1884). Czech music—born of years of tyranny, the Thirty Years' War, Hapsburg domination, Germanization, and eventually "freedom"—could not be repressed any more than its people could.

Smetana, who lived and died in Bohemia, was dedicated to his country and to music. After taking part in the fiery Revolution of 1848, which was short-lived, he opened a music school in Prague. From then on he concentrated his life and all his efforts on creating a style and a music that were distinctly Czech. The first of his patriotic operas was called *The Brandenburgs in Bohemia* (1863). The joyous approval it received was pale acceptance compared to that of his second opera, *The Bartered Bride* (1866). This opera with its colorful Bohemian melodies and its spirited national rhythms has become popular all over the world. It is doubtful, though, that its very rustic, Czech good humor has been authentically captured in performances outside of the country of its birth. Alien singers and producers have a way of substituting slapstick for genial Czech comedy.

Like Mozart, Smetana was a child prodigy, and his music has been compared to Mozart's for its spontaneous warmth and good-humored frankness. *The Kiss* (1876), *The Secret* (1878), two more comedies, and two serious patriotic operas, *Dalibor* (1868) and *Libussa* (1872), are still performed in Czechoslovakia and at festivals throughout Europe by the renowned National Theater of Prague.

The fires of Czech nationalism were kept burning by Antonín Dvořák (1841–1904). He was born into a poor and simple family, and for a while it looked as though his musical gifts would be smothered by the necessities of working in his father's butcher shop. Luckily, a farsighted and warmhearted schoolmaster—the kind one reads of in old novels—saw to it that Antonín received the proper education and direction that enabled him to become one of the finest composers, conductors, and teachers of the nineteenth century.

His international fame rests mainly with his magnificent orchestral works and songs, especially his *Symphony from the New World,* but several of the ten operas he composed were popular in his native land. *Rusalka* (1901) is probably his finest theatrical achievement.

Another Czech composer, Jaromir Weinberger (1896–1967) wrote *Schwanda the Bagpiper.* At its premiere in 1927 it gave evidence of becoming a rival to *The Bartered Bride.* However, its popularity has not truly extended itself outside of Prague, and it has not been heard in America since 1931.

Czechoslovakia's major composer during the early twentieth century was Leoš Janáček (1854–1928). As is typical of unusual men with unusual ideas, Janáček's dramatic opera *Jenufa* was ignored at its premiere in Brno, 1904. Twelve years later, audiences in Prague declared it a masterpiece. *Jenufa's* music and the bittersweet story of a young girl and her illegitimate child were called amateurish when it was first performed in New York in 1924. Subsequent performances in Chicago (1959) with the great Dutch soprano, Gré Brouwenstijn, in the title role, and in New York (1966), were hailed as deeply moving. The latter, a concert performance, was conducted by

Thomas Scherman. His cast of gifted American singers had learned their roles in the original Czech. Scherman's important decision to present the opera as it had been intended by its composer undoubtedly gave new insight into Janáček's musical genius—for the simple reason that all of Janáček's music is based on the cadence and inflections of the Czech language.

Katya Kabanová (1921) was Janáček's next opera. It is a dramatic work of great poignancy and carries his idea of music "born of words" even farther. *The Cunning Little Vixen* (1924) is a delightful nature opera that tells the story of a clever fox showing a blustering game warden the real meaning of life. That it has never been given a professional stage performance in America is a minor tragedy. Once it has been seen and heard in a striking production like the one at the National Theater in Prague, one realizes that *The Vixen* is a masterpiece of its kind equal to Ravel's *L'enfant et les sortilèges* (*The Child and the Sorceries*) (1925). Both show the same originality and the same capacity for creating a believable and still magic world of animals and humans, showing how nature binds them together.

The Makropulos Case (1926), based on Čapek's bizarre play, was given its first American performance in San Francisco in 1967. The complicated plot deals with a court trial that has dragged on for many years. More complications arise with the appearance of the leading lady, Emilia Marty, whom we later discover has lived for more than three hundred years. She is searching for an elixir, given her by her father as an experiment. Until the action of the opera begins, this secret has kept her eternally young and beautiful. The leading exponent of this musically and dramatically taxing role is Marie Collier, the Australian soprano.

Janáček's last opera is a depressing, but intense and original, setting of Dostoyevsky's detailed account of his life in Siberia. Entitled *From the House of the Dead* (1928), it has yet to be performed in the United States.

Despite the condemnation of critics and their suggestions that Janáček's operas should never have left the forests and hills of Moravia, they have proved their right to live. Forty years after his death, jet-age audiences are discovering that his works are more than nationalistic Bohemian operas, limited in their enjoyment to the people of one country. They are the product of an original and provocative mind that was young and creative to the day it died—at seventy-four.

CHAPTER FIFTEEN

Down with Tradition

A devastating "little" World War (1914–1918) was responsible for musical as well as political and sociological changes. Postwar musicians, the spokesmen for angry and exhausted civilizations, began a new war against tradition. Rebellion and change became the loud and clear words of the day. They were words strengthened by memories and years of deprivation and death. Once more composers were asking the perennial and debatable question: Isn't musical art intended as a reflection and expression solely of the contemporary?

If one accepts an affirmative answer, one must admit that the new and dissonant sounds created by tradition-defying composers of the 1920s and '30s are the expressive and acceptable means for creating music that will live. If, on the other hand, one is inclined to agree with Romain Rolland that "music accommodates itself to the characters of all people and all time. Art is humanity's dream—a dream of light and liberty and quiet power," then one might respond to new and contemporary music with some negativism.

There is no doubt that new experiments in opera are valid

and that they are honest expressions from the souls of serious musicians. They remain, with few exceptions, limited in their communicative powers and negligible in their persuasion at the box office. These experiments, successful and not so successful, must be given attention. Also we must not forget that history has been quick to catalogue the names of composers whose new music was ugly only because audiences had not become familiar with it. Perhaps the day will come, as Paul Henry Lang has suggested in the *New York Herald Tribune,* when "overalls, bicycles, and cocktails will seem as natural and familiar on the operatic stage as are armor, swan-drawn barges and love potions." Let us look at some of the composers who were determined to be different.

Igor Stravinsky (1882–   ) is considered by some a forceful musician of the twentieth century. He is admired and imitated. He is hated and dismissed.

Vernon Duke, in his book *Listen Here!* slaughters the man and his music. Robert Craft, an American conductor and authority on Stravinsky, in several volumes elevates him to the realm of deities. You may listen to his music and make your decison.

Stravinsky was born in Russia and studied law before becoming an orchestration pupil of the great Rimsky-Korsakov. The pupil was later to criticize the master by saying: "There was nothing profound either in Rimsky's nature or in his music. He was sometimes shockingly shallow in his artistic aims." That the world knows otherwise is comment enough.

After he completed his university studies, Stravinsky journeyed to Paris where he fell in with the musical elite. His *Fantastic Scherzo* brought him to the attention of the great impresario, Serge Diaghilev. Diaghilev's stupendous Ballet Russe Company was overwhelming Paris with voluptuous ballet productions, and Stravinsky desired to overwhelm the city in another way—with his new "shocking" music for *Le Sacre du printemps* (*The Rite of Spring*) (1913). His novel, clashing dissonances and his blaring climaxes with instruments burning their way through the orchestral fabric in direct opposition to one another created a near riot. The audience stormed out of the theater.

The controversial and complex composer's musical life encompasses many changes. With his *opera buffa, Mavra* (1922), he discarded the percussive shock techniques of his famous ballets and started on a "new" road. His compositions of this new phase are spoken of as the "neo-classic" period, and have been called "the ultimate in the dehumanization of music."

His opera *The Rake's Progress* (1951) is a Stravinskian attempt to write a traditional eighteenth-century opera. Many scholarly musicians accept it as a major work of art. The public stays away. Stravinsky remains one of the most feted, publicized, and wealthy composers of the century.

An artistic theory of expressionism sprang up during and following World War I which claimed that its aims were to create an *expression* of the artist's emotional reactions instead of the representation of the natural appearance of objects and people.

Arnold Schoenberg (1874–1951) was born in Vienna, and his painting, rather than his music, brought him into contact with expressionist painter Wassilly Kandinsky. One can compare Schoenberg's short operas, *Erwartung* (*Expectation*) (1909) and *Die Glückliche Hand* (*The Lucky Hand*) (1913), to expressionist canvases. Their harmonies are colorful, dissonant, and thick with notes. Their plots are odd and symbolic.

A third short opera, *Von Heute auf Morgen* (*From Today Until Tomorrow*) (1930) is fifty minutes of comedy and twelve-tone technique. Twelve-tone is a musical term describing a technique of composing in which all the twelve notes that make up an octave (the seven white and five black notes of the piano) are used "equally" and are subject to a relationship of strict order.

In 1933, when his works were listed as degenerate by the Nazis, he came to the United States, became a citizen and taught until his death. Prior to that, in 1930–32, he had completed the libretto and music for two acts of a monumental theater work, *Moses und Aron*. The third act of this truly profound tragedy was never completed. Schoenberg took his story from Exodus. Its theme of faith and the struggle between action and wisdom was close to the composer's heart and intellect.

Moses und Aron is a combination of opera and oratorio. Its chorus music has been compared to Bach and Handel for grandeur, its solo scenes to Wagner for psychological power, and its orchestral virtuosity to Stravinsky. American audiences did not see *Moses und Aron* until 1966. These performances in Boston, under the dynamic and enterprising guidance of Sara Caldwell, made music history and—incomplete or not—cheering audiences and less demonstrative critics agreed that it was one of the masterpieces of the century.

Schoenberg's pupil Alban Berg (1885–1935) followed in the twelve-tone path of his teacher. His *Wozzeck* (1925) is a nightmare music drama that paints a picture of German postwar bitterness and neuroses with a musical scalpel and dabs of blood. The opera is atonal, or not in any key, and its hero, Wozzeck, is an unfortunate clod of a soldier who is taken advantage of by everyone. Georg Büchner, the author, never intended that Wozzeck be accepted as just a tormented fool. He is a symbol of man who is trapped by destiny and can do nothing to save himself from the murderous intentions of men who do not care.

The opera builds with the tension of a taut steel wire to the scene in which the hero murders his mistress. *Wozzeck* closes with music and a dramatic situation that are devastating in their impact. Wozzeck has committed suicide, and we see his little boy, riding a hobbyhorse, alone in the public square, as his friends dash off to see his mother's body.

Wozzeck has marched determinedly through a stormy career. Riots broke out at the premiere in Berlin, but the opera chalked up almost forty performances before the Nazi rise to power in 1933 made any more presentations impossible. The Czechs who heard it in 1926 created such violent scenes of protest that it was withdrawn from the National Theater. Its first American performances were in Philadelphia and New York in 1931. New Yorkers heard it again in 1951—a concert performance conducted by Dimitri Mitropoulos. In 1952 the New York City Opera staged an English language version with one of the great Wozzecks, Marko Rothmüller. The Met bravely decided to present *Wozzeck* in 1959!

About every two years *Wozzeck* takes another stand and hypnotically increases its hold on American audiences. The great Karl Böhm conducted a strong revival at the Metropolitan (1964) with William Dooley as the hapless Wozzeck and the superb singing actress, Helga Pilarczyk, as Marie. In 1969 Evelyn Lear was Marie and the brilliant English conductor Colin Davis was on the podium.

Berg's next opera, *Lulu* (1935), is an uncompleted work. The composer died before he could finish orchestrating the third act. Its brutal atonality, *Sprechstimme* a German term for speech-song, halfway between speech and song created by Schoenberg; the singer touches the note but does not sustain it, and spoken dialogue, interspersed with sections of startling lyricism—bring one of the most unremittingly evil women of all opera to life. They are vivid examples of methods composers like Berg felt compelled to use in order that they could truthfully express the desperate and horrible moods of the time.

Lulu was premiered in Zurich, 1937. It was finally heard in the United States in 1965, at the War Memorial Opera House in San Francisco, where the American soprano, Evelyn Lear, who is considered one of the major interpreters of Lulu, sang the title role.

Miss Lear writes about *Lulu* most interestingly: "As has often been said, Lulu is the incarnation of uninhibited womanhood. But, just as obviously, she is—objectively considered—loathsome and criminal. How can one take such an 'unsympathetic' character and make her, artistically speaking, sympathetic? That was my problem with Lulu.

"One has, I think, to present Lulu as helpless by nature. Adoration is a phenomenon which, to her, is as natural as her own being. She is sort of a puppet on which the real world impinges. And yet she feels—and Berg marvellously expresses it in his music—real pain, real sorrow, real love for her 'puppet-master,' Dr. Schoen.

"I think of her as a sort of sensual Eliza Doolittle, formed and *made* by another's hand. She has the innocence of Eve and the cunning of a child."

That audiences are showing their increasing interest in *Wozzeck* is a favorable sign for *Lulu*. The lurid story and often grotesque music, accepted as it is by many, does not appeal to the mass of operagoers, particularly in America. That it is a milestone of modern music, there is little doubt. However, there are some who believe the expressionist-horror story deserves the fate of its heroine. Her throat was slit by Jack the Ripper!

Composers in France were breaking traditions too. Arthur Honegger, Darius Milhaud, Francis Poulenc, Georges Auric, Germaine Tailleferre, and Louis Durey declared themselves and their break from anything resembling the nebulousness of impressionism by organizing "Les Six" ("The Six").

Like many French get-togethers, "The Six" had an abundance of individual charm and talent to amuse but not a great deal of group force. Personally and collectively they were spellbound by the musical wit and independence of their mentor, Erik Satie (1886–1925)—possibly even more so by the astonishing machinations of the multitalented *enfant terrible* Jean Cocteau. Except for Honegger (1892–1955) the influence of both of these men is visible in the music of "Les Six."

Honegger was born in France, but his formal Swiss heritage is evident in some of his classic ideas and his admiration for Bach and Lully. Honegger's *Le Roi David* (*King David*) (1921) is an opera-oratorio. Its success in Paris established him as a composer of importance. His gifts for writing powerful choral music are displayed in both *Judith* (1926) and *Antigone* (1927). *Antigone* with its dissonance and its insistent, percussive rhythms is something of a forerunner of another musical experiment utilizing the same play by Sophocles— Carl Orff's *Antigonae* (1949).

One of Honegger's most effective stage works is *Jeanne d'Arch au Bûcher* (*Joan of Arc at the Stake*) (1938). The poetic drama requires large forces for presentation: actors, singers, both an adult and a children's chorus, and full orchestra. The title role has intrigued famous actresses from Ida Rubinstein to Ingrid Bergman. The film actress made her debut at La Scala in this work.

Darius Milhaud (1892–   ) is a composer whose musical gifts are as varied as Joseph's coat was colored. He refused to be limited to any style or category and his opera-oratorios, his heroic operas, his comic operas, and his short-short operas (written as sort of a jab at Wagner's "never-ending" dramas) show remarkable evidence of his being able to write in any idiom. Diplomatic service in Brazil made him a devotee of popular South American dances, and time he spent in the United States introduced him to jazz, which he believed was the salvation of musical art.

His ballet for Negroes, *La Création du Monde* (*The Creation of the World*) (1923), is an example of his clever and original musicality. This work combines the best of jazz *and* Bach!

Le Pauvre Matelot (*The Poor Sailor*) (1926), his first major operatic success, has melodious tongue-in-cheek music that is perfectly wedded to a theatrical Jean Cocteau text about a not-too-clever sailor who is murdered by his own wife when he returns after a long absence and tells her he is the wealthy friend of her penniless mate.

Milhaud's epic opera, *Christophe Colomb,* was premiered in Berlin, 1930. The drama was written by Paul Claudel, one of the masters of French literature, and it is a combination of opera, Greek drama, mystery play, film technique, and musical-philosophical debate.

Christophe Colomb was followed by *Maximilien* (1932), *Médée* (1940—its premiere was interrupted by the Nazi occupation of Paris), *Bolivar* (1943), and *David* (1954).

Francis Poulenc (1899–1963) was a clever, witty, and sophisticated composer who was as theatrically alert as his colleague Cocteau. The beautiful people and the opera world raised an eyebrow, smiled cagily at the suggestive surrealistic text for his *Les Mamelles de Tirésias* (*The Breasts of Tiresias*) (1947) and spontaneously acclaimed his telling and intentionally vulgar music.

In 1957 Poulenc's *Les Dialogues des Carmelites* (*The Dialogues of the Carmelites*) attracted a packed house of admirers and critics. The first performance took place at La Scala, Milan—in Italian—and the Paris Opéra hailed it—sung in French—later in the year. Audiences who were expecting scintillating, transparent musical effects for effect's sake remained in their seats and applauded a truly poetic opera that shows possibilities of taking its place in the repertory of opera houses throughout the world. The libretto of the *Dialogues* was adapted from a novel by Gertrude von Le Fort. The story is about a young woman of the nobility who joins the Carmelite order and is trapped and persecuted by the Revolutionary terrorists. It has impressed audiences in Germany, England, the United States (including via television), and in Austria.

The role of Blanche de la Force has been sung by Virginia Zeani, Denise Duval, Dorothy Kirsten, Gabriella Tucci, and Irmgard Seefreid—fine sopranos and actresses every one.

The world premiere of Poulenc's one-character opera, *La Voix Humaine* (*The Human Voice*), took place in Paris in 1959. Cocteau's melodramatic tour de force of a woman bidding farewell to her lover—on the telephone—was given added dimension by Poulenc's skillful, romantic music. Denise Duval was the unnamed heroine—She—at the premiere. Later, her striking performance was repeated in New York City.

German-born Paul Hindemith (1895–1963) was, like Milhaud, a craftsman with a mastery of several styles. Unlike the Frenchman, his prolific outpouring of music strikes many as ponderous—like the word that is synonymous with his name —*Gebrauchmusik*. A literal translation is "useful music." It is obvious in much of Hindemith's music that too much usefulness can be as sleep-provoking as too much good taste. Fortunately he retracted some of his dogmatic demands as time went on.

Hindemith's *Mathis der Maler* (*Mathias the Painter*) (1938) is an opera-oratorio composed in his later polyphonic style. Its seven scenes tell the story of a sixteenth-century painter and his conflict of ideals—should man be true to art and himself or take arms for a cause he has no faith in. *Die Harmonie der Welt* (*The Harmony of the Universe*) (1957) is a massive opera in fourteen scenes. Despite sections of striking beauty and craftsmanship, the characters of the drama rarely come to

life. One is eventually left with the impression of having listened to expertly outlined philosophical and musical ideas but
of having been moved or touched not at all.

The Socialist Revolution in Russia may have liberated the
people, but it imprisoned her composers by forcing them to
write "Soviet" music. Conventional "Russian" music was allowed—"Western" music and anything suggesting dissonance
or the bourgeois ideas of Hindemith and Schoenberg became a
crime against the state.

One of the most notable of Soviet operas is *The Quiet Don*
by Ivan Dzerzhinsky. It is a propaganda opera that met all the
requirements set down by the Union of Soviet Composers, and
its premiere in Leningrad (1935) was blessed by the approval
and personal appearance of Stalin.

This public acceptance by the Soviet leader was another way
of castigating the brilliant—and up until this time admired—
Dimitri Shostakovich (1906–   ) who had made the dangerous error of writing a lurid opera, *Lady Macbeth of Mtzensk*
(1934), which contained not only much frowned-upon unme-
lodic music but a leading lady who was degenerate and embarrassing to the ideals of the state. Strangely enough, *Lady
Macbeth* was greeted with proletarian approval at its first Leningrad performance. Subsequent performances in New York,
Cleveland, and Cincinnati were to prove that Shostakovich's
grim melodrama was also a commodity greatly admired by
capitalist audiences. *That* sin could not be forgiven. *Pravda*
lashed out at the composer and his works as being "a leftist
mess," and *Lady Macbeth* was not heard again in Russia until
1962. By that time Shostakovich had written his *Fifth Sym-*

phony and proved he had seen the error of his musical ways. The 1962 version of *Lady Macbeth* was called *Katerina Izmailova,* and it has had highly acclaimed performances in London, New York, and San Francisco.

Soviet Russia's outstanding composer is Sergei Prokofiev (1891–1953). Mozartean in his precocity, he wrote his first opera when he was six! His music glows and bites with satire and wit.

The Love for Three Oranges (1921), one of his most popular successes, was given its first performance in Chicago, and since its 1949 production by the New York City Opera it has become a part of that company's permanent repertoire.

His *The Flaming Angel* was performed for the first time at the Venice Festival of 1955. Its hysterical heroine, Renata, and its fantastic sixteenth-century plot did about as much for Prokofiev in the way of gaining state approval and admiration as *Katerina* had for Shostakovich. His *opera buffa, The Duenna* (1946), is accepted more approvingly. The year 1955 marked the Leningrad premiere of his heroic and monumental *War and Peace.* The first version of the opera, which is based on the epic novel of Leo Tolstoy, was given in 1946. The Western world heard a cut version in Florence, 1953. Rare is the opera company—except the Bolshoi in Moscow—that can afford a production of the work. It has a cast of seventy-two solo singers!

As visitors to Expo '67, Montreal, know, Russia has kept the glorious traditional splendors of opera and ballet alive. She also has performing musicians such as Sviatoslav Richter, Emil Gilels, David Oistrakh; virtuoso singers like Galina Vishneveskaya and Zara Doulakanova; the legendary dancers, Galina Ulanova and Maya Plisetskaya, who prove that her days of greatness are far from over.

Unfortunately, the iron hand of state did much to stifle anything that might be daring and original in her composers. Those who resisted did it meekly. Others apologized. Perhaps now they will take courage from her writers and poets. Russian opera may not have died.

Carl Orff (1895–   ) is a vigorous experimenter. The German composer, at seventy-three, is still resisting the established forms and traditions of Occidental music. His *Carmina Burana* (1937) brought him international attention, and thirty years later it is still a popular and provocative item in the repertory of many opera houses throughout the world. This work was followed by *Catulli Carmina* (1943) and *Trionfo di Aphrodite* (*The Triumph of Aphrodite*) (1953). All three are basically cantatas with dance and spoken dialogue. In 1949 Orff completed the first work of a theater trilogy that is intended to be the musical testament to his beliefs that music must elaborate and add to the spoken (and sometimes sung) word. Orff feels this form is the only possibility open for the modern composer. The most natural way to achieve this intentionally primitive style of theater work was to go to Greek tragedy. Orff selected Hölderlin's adaptation of Sophocles' *Antigone* for his first major world-theater work. Audiences at the 1949 Salzburg Festival were not certain if Orff's bizarre orchestra—six pianos, four harps, string basses, batteries of percussion instruments, gongs, and castanets—made beautiful music, but the text of the drama was admittedly heightened by the persistent musical rhythms and sudden crescendos of shattering sound. Critics found the work lacking in imagination and melody. At *Antigonae's* American premiere, in New York City's Philharmonic Hall (The Little Orchestra Society, 1968) it was greeted with a standing ovation and critics decided that it was an enduring and memorable work of art.

Oedipus der Tyrann (*Oedipus the Tyrant*) (1959) is a somewhat shorter work and consequently does not make such demands of concentration on its audience. The final part of the trilogy, *Prometheus,* had its world premiere in Stuttgart, Germany, in March, 1968. Considering that Orff's music dramas are primarily concerned with the power of the *words,* his singers must have not only a command of half-speech, chant, and regular speech—but also the ability to sing difficult intervals—and be superb actors.

Carlos Alexander, an American baritone who has been very successful in European opera houses, is considered the leading exponent of Orff's unusual theater experiments. Mr. Alexander is a prime example of what a great singing actor is.

It would be difficult to mention all the others who have resisted and broken with tradition. But there were others, too.

Gottfried von Einem, an Austrian, has made strong impressions with his *Dantons Tod* (*Danton's Death*) (1947) and *Der Prozess* (*The Trial*) (1953); Rolf Liebermann, Swiss composer, attracted serious attention with his *L'ecole des Femmes* (*The School for Wives,*) and another Swiss, Frank Martin, has written two atmospheric and original operas, a Tristan and Isolde setting entitled *Le Vin Herbe* (*The Herb Wine*) and *The Storm.* Among Italian operatic composers mention must be made of Ildebrando Pizzetti, whose *Assassinio nella Cattedrale* (*Murder in the Cathedral*) (1958), based on T. S. Eliot's play, brought him to international attention. Pizzetti was then seventy-seven. Luigi Dallapiccola is another. His *Il Prigioniero* (*The Prisoner*) (1949) has been performed in Italy and the United States. Its twelve-tone, autonomous music has caused heated arguments and critical discussions.

More recent are the late Karl-Birger Blomdahl, Hans Werner Henze, and Gunther Schuller.

Blomdahl died in Sweden in June of 1968. He was an eclectic composer who was influenced early in his career by the music of Paul Hindemith. His operas were a combination of electronic music, serial methods, and "popular" songs. He was brought to international attention with the premiere of his space opera, *Aniara* (1959) just a couple of years after the Russians had sent Sputnik I into the atmsophere. Its strong, provocative plot deals with 8,000 passengers on a spaceship, all under the power of a computer, who discover that the ship has gone off its planned course and there is nothing ahead of them but death.

He was working on another opera, *The Saga of the Super Computer,* when he died. He was a very pessimistic man and once commented: "I want to shake people, to awaken them to the reality of catastrophes that are closer than they think."

The German composer Henze was born in 1926, and he has lived in Italy since the early '50s. He also is a twelve-tone exponent. His operas include *Boulevard Solitude*—a modern *Manon* (1952), *Elegy for Young Lovers* (1961), *Der junge lord* (*The Young Lord*) (1965), and *The Bassarids* (1966).

Henze does not like to think of opera as a popular entertainment, and he believes that the stage sets, the lights, and the acting are only added means of explaining the music. His music is complex and occasionally traditional. His operatic innovations are most apparent in his writing for the voice. Here everything is "new"—at least new in the sense of acknowledging Schoenberg and Boulez.

American audiences heard *The Bassarids* during the summer of 1968 when the daring and imaginative Santa Fe Opera Company presented it in its brand-new theater, the other having been completely destroyed during a mysterious fire in 1967.

The American Gunther Schuller (1925–) is a twelve-tone musician who is also a superb horn player. He was a member of the Metropolitan Opera orchestra for fifteen years and is now the president of the New England Conservatory of Music.

The various "successes" of his three-act opera, *The Visitation* (1966), are examples of the transitional times we live in. At its premiere in Hamburg, Germany, it was greeted with critical and audience approval. When the same company presented the work in the Metropolitan Opera House in 1967, its Kafka-esque libretto set to music in the twelve-tone idiom, plus jazz and blues, was welcomed with boos at the final curtain. The New York critics were also not impressed. But several months later, in San Francisco, the opera was received with a genuine ovation!

There, in brief, are the major innovators and the men of experiment. Some who resisted tradition survived—others were silenced by governments and the tragedy that time was not ready for them.

CHAPTER SIXTEEN

Several Americans – and One Britten

That opera—and music in general—got a foot in the door during the early pages of American history is nothing less than miraculous. Scarlatti and Rameau may have been enchanting European music lovers but the hardy, puritanical settlers in the New World would have no truck with such unholy and immoral indulgences. Prima donnas who were trilling away in London and Venice as they drove poets and diplomats to duels at sunrise would have been tarred and feathered had they set foot in the colonies. Fortunately for opera lovers and, indeed, the musical culture of the United States, the more broadminded Virginians had the courage to present a ballad opera there in the 1730s.

By that time, New Orleans was greeting adventurous Frenchmen and later inviting opera stars to appear in its famous theater, *Le Spectacle de la Rue St. Pierre.*

New York City began playing host to small theater companies and their ballad operas, just about the time the Continental Congress slapped a ban on anything resembling public entertainment. Philadelphians braved the scorn of the hierarchy and managed to have a theater and a musical season that lasted for six months during 1759. They weren't strong enough, though, for the narrow-minded Pennsylvania government immediately outlawed opera for the next eight years. Things began to look up in the 1820s, and New Yorkers decided that they really enjoyed works like Bishop's *Clari, the Maid of Milan* and Weber's *Der Freischütz.*

With the arrival in the United States of the flamboyant García family in 1825, opera and opera singers saw signs of being accepted with some friendliness. At least they were no longer regarded as works and creatures of the Devil. How and why American composers started composing is a matter of conjecture, but it is certain the first real opera by an American was written by William Henry Fry (1813-1864). He was an outspoken and articulate gentleman who deplored anything tainted by the word "European," especially European composers. Ferociously American or not, Mr. Fry's *Leonora* (1845) has overtones of Meyerbeer.

Since the Swedish Nightingale, Jenny Lind, was touring the United States and Cuba under the shrewd aegis of P. T. Barnum around this time, her voice and his showmanship must be given credit for whetting the operatic appetites of some Americans. Lind's two or three seasons in the States made opera and its arias almost as popular as Tom Thumb, the legendary midget.

George Frederick Bristow's *Rip Van Winkle* (1855) is, despite its dubious worth, the second American opera we know of.

By the early 1800s, music had taken a giant step forward with the formation of the first orchestra in the United States

—the Boston Philharmonic Society. Considering that just 135 years before, our ancestors had laws forbidding any instruments but the trumpet and drum to be played, we were showing signs of progress.

The great and revered Walter Damrosch (1862–1950) was a gifted composer who was also dedicated to educating the public and making it aware of the value of music and its importance to every society. His first opera, *The Scarlet Letter* (1896), was a genuine success. *Cyrano de Bergerac* appeared in 1913, and *The Man Without a Country,* in 1937. This opera is notable more for the fact that the golden-voiced Helen Traubel was in the cast rather than for its romantic German, nineteenth-century melodic traits. Helen Traubel became one of the Met's leading Wagnerian artists. Later in her career her public disagreements with Rudolf Bing, general manager of the Metropolitan Opera, over her desire to perform in nightclubs resulted in her departure from that house.

Damrosch's last opera was *The Opera Cloak* in 1942.

Henry K. Hadley (1871–1937), Horatio Parker (1863–1919), and Richard Hageman (1882–1966) were American composers whose works all reached the stage of the Metropolitan Opera, but none of them are heard today.

Deems Taylor (1885–1966) was a composer with true melodic gifts. He was also a man of charm and wit. His many writings and radio programs amused and educated the public up until the time of his death.

When his opera *The King's Henchman,* had its world premiere at the Met (1927), the learned critic Olin Downes wrote: "But it has undeniably theatrical effect, conciseness, movement, youthful spirit and sincerity . . . it is clear that

Mr. Taylor and Miss Millay have produced the most effectively and artistically wrought American opera that has reached the stage."

The libretto was by Edna St. Vincent Millay (1892–1950), the amazing American whose poems written in the 1920s caused a storm of protest and admiration. Her "liberated" ideas about love and morals and her beautiful lyric poetry made her one of the most celebrated and successful poets of the century.

Taylor's *Peter Ibbetson* was first heard in 1931. The famous actress Constance Collier wrote the libretto which was based on a romantic fantasy by George du Maurier. Critics have complained that it is watered down Debussy and Wagner. It isn't. Its lovely, lyric music deserves more than the too few hearings it has had.

Another important American opera is *Merry Mount* (1934) by Howard Hanson (1896–). It was one of the fifteen American operas presented by General Manager Giulio Gatti-Casazza during his tenure as director of the Metropolitan Opera.

There is a consensus that America's real claim to musical fame is the musical comedy—not opera. Before considering the modern musical comedy and/or musical play it is useful to know what preceded them. Victor Herbert (1859–1924) wrote melodic operettas like *Babes in Toyland, Mlle Modiste,* and *Naughty Marietta.* These and many more Herbert operettas played to "standing room only" houses for years. They also became movies that made musical and financial history during the '30s. Today there are many "old-timers" past thirty who stay up to catch a rerun of *Naughty Marietta*—with Jeanette MacDonald and Nelson Eddy—on T.V. One of the great music critics of our time, Claudia Cassidy, points out in reviews that Miss MacDonald was more than a movie star. She was a first-rate singer and her performances of Juliette in *Roméo et Juliette* and Marguerite in *Faust* (Chicago, Montreal, and Cincinnati—1944) proved it. She had a solid technique, striking flexibility, and a winning vocal quality. She was also one of the few Americans with a sense of the true French style.

Viennese composers Franz Lehár, Oscar Straus, and Rudolf Friml made fortunes with their appealing operettas, several of which are performed today. Friml's *Rose Marie* and *The Vagabond King* haven't fared so well, but Lehár's' *The Merry Widow* is still attracting audiences. In New York and on the road, just two years ago, former Metropolitan opera soprano Patrice Munsel, proved that Lehár's melodies are practically timeless. Miss Munsel made her debut at the Met in December of 1943. She was eighteen and the youngest artist in Metropolitan history to sing a leading role in that theater.

Straus's *The Chocolate Soldier* was extremely popular for more than thirty years. And his *A Waltz Dream* (1907), which introduced the beautiful tenor voice of Edward Johnson to the American public, was revived in a concert performance at New York's Lincoln Center in 1968!

Jerome Kern (1885–1945) was one of the greatest of light opera composers. Some people call his *Show Boat* nothing more than a musical comedy, but whatever category you decide to put it in, it is a masterpiece. Its songs have become more than "standards"—they are classics. *Show Boat* is revived every year. To hear William Warfield sing "Ol' Man River," and radiant Jean Sanders (a fine Carmen, by the way) sing "Bill" and "Can't Help Lovin' that Man" is reason enough for a revival. Kern wrote dozens of superb musical comedies and operettas, including *Roberta* which introduced not only Bob Hope to big-time audiences but also a nostalgic song, "Yesterdays," that is still sung all over the world.

The prolific Cole Porter wrote both the words and music for his sophisticated musical comedies. His overwhelming successes are too numerous to mention, but after considering that *Kiss Me, Kate* has been heard in every major city of the world since its first performance in 1948, we should pay some tribute to just a few of its witty and melodic songs. "Wunderbar," "Always True to You in My Fashion," "So in Love," and "Were Thine that Special Face" show no evidence today of beginning to tire the public. Later a famous *Salome,* Brenda Lewis, appeared in *Kate* at its Viennese premiere!

Although she makes no pretense about being a *bel canto* singer, Ethel Merman has been a musical comedy star for many years. Her unique characterizations, particularly in *Annie Get Your Gun* and *Gypsy,* are memorable in theater annals.

Too many words have been written about how *Oklahoma!* revolutionized the American musical theater in the '40s. It is a part of musical history, though, and it was the beginning of a long and fruitful collaboration between Richard Rodgers and his librettist, Oscar Hammerstein II. Their *South Pacific* won a Pulitzer Prize in 1950 and made a matinee idol out of an opera star—Ezio Pinza. This magnificent Don Giovanni was also a magnificent Émile de Becque.

The incomparable Gertrude Lawrence raised Rodgers and Hammerstein's superb *The King and I* to the level of a minor masterpiece. The score is Rodgers at his best and Hammerstein at his top form. His book and lyrics illuminated thoughts and used words with tender care. *The King and I* never lapses into the maudlin sentimentality that burdened some of their later collaborations—like *The Sound of Music.*

When Frank Loesser's *Guys and Dolls* opened in 1950, it was subtitled *A Musical Fable of Broadway.* Louis Untermeyer verifies that it was more than a musical comedy. He called it: ". . . an operatic jamboree, Verdi in terms of Times Square. Everything about it was extraordinary.'"

The indefatigable conductor, composer, writer, Leonard Bernstein gave the theater *On the Town, Wonderful Town,* the brilliant but ill-fated *Candide,* and *West Side Story.*

My Fair Lady remains a spectacular and unquestioned glory of the American musical theater. Its lilting melodies have been translated and heard in every capital of the world, making its creators millionaires.

All these works and these composers bring us to a point that evidently must be argued about by all healthy opera buffs and musical comedy lovers: but isn't opera *better* than musical comedy?

Isn't this a snobbish and empty inquiry? They can both be enjoyed, and they can both bring something to the listener. One can agree with the late critic Robert Sabin and his beliefs that "the composer of opera approaches his theme with a far greater and more demanding musical technique than the composer of musicals, and that his aesthetic purpose is different." But one may also disagree with him somewhat that the musical "almost always founders when it attempts genuine tragedy on its own terms."

It is agreed that musical comedy is basically "entertainment."

But in recent years the musical has tried—and often successfully —to inject moments of serious thought and power into its entertaining framework. Genuine tragic moments they may not be, but they are, nonetheless, moving, thought-provoking, and—to many—sources of inspiration. *West Side Story* has moments like this. As do *The King and I, The Fantasticks, Most Happy Fella, Cabaret, Fiddler on the Roof,* and most certainly *The Man of La Mancha.*

Opera could use some of Broadway's outspokenness and stage virtuosity. And some opera singers could use some musical-play acting techniques. On the other hand, Broadway could use more good voices to sing some of its more memorable music. Things got out of hand with Rex Harrison's *Sprechstimme* in *My Fair Lady;* and they continue going downhill as far as singing is concerned.

But rather than compare and denounce either one or the other, why not enjoy them both? No matter what its dissenters would have us believe, American musical comedy has not killed opera. It is alive and well and living in many cities throughout the world.

So, happily, are *Mame, Hello, Dolly!* and *Funny Girl.*

George Gershwin (1898–1937) completed his opera, *Porgy and Bess,* in 1935, and the leading singers at its premiere were Todd Duncan and Anne Brown. Although many refer to it as a "folk opera," when their real purpose is to dismiss it as a musical comedy, it has no folk songs in it. Gershwin did borrow from jazz and Negro spirituals for his expressive songs like "My Man's Gone," "Summertime," and "Bess, You Is My Woman," but *Porgy* can proudly retain its right to be called an opera.

Its lengthy tour of the United States and Europe in the '50s brought the extraordinary soprano Leontyne Price to international attention. Her subsequent TV performances of *The Magic Flute* and *Tosca* made her a major prima donna, and for the past ten years she has been a much-sought-after singer at all the leading opera houses.

The Metropolitan's general manager, Rudolf Bing, has many enemies who continue to argue his policy. Let us say his career at that theater has been notable if only for his superb productions of *Don Carlo* and *The Woman Without a Shadow*—and his imagination in introducing Negro singers to that house.

The first was the great contralto, Marian Anderson, who wrote: "The chance to be a member of the Metropolitan has been a highlight of my life. It has meant much to me and my people. If I have been privileged to serve as a symbol, to be the first Negro to sing as a regular member of the company, I take greater pride from knowing that it has encouraged other singers of my group to realize that the doors everywhere may open increasingly to those who have prepared themselves well."

Other black artists who have become an important part of the international opera scene include: the late Ellabelle Davis, a superb *Aïda* in this country and at La Scala; Mattiwilda Dobbs, a scintillating coloratura who is a remarkable Gilda and *Zerbinetta;* the late Lawrence Winters, a memorable *Rigoletto*. Leonora Lafayette is, like Camilla Williams, a fine *Butterfly*. Two young artists who graduated from musical comedy to become prima donnas are Gloria Davy and Reri Grist. George Shirley is a leading tenor with opera companies throughout the world. Margaret Tynes is a superb *Salome* and a magnificent *Lady Macbeth;* Shirley Verrett has been heard in England and Russia as well as the United States. Ella Lee, Grace Bumbry, Martina Arroyo, and Felicia Weathers are also divas in the truest sense of the word.

Miss Price's glorious voice and artistry were put to something of a test when she was given the honor of heading the cast for the opening night in the Metropolitan's new home in Lincoln Center. The opera was Samuel Barber's (1910–) *Antony and Cleopatra.* Only a real professional could have surmounted the burdens of the occasion. The music was negligible, the script and the staging were pompous, and she was stuck inside a huge golden sphinx for interminable minutes. *Cleopatra* has been dropped from the repertoire.

Barber's *Vanessa* (1958) is a fine theater piece with some opportunities for real singing. An orchestral interlude and a quintet are particularly lovely. On hearing *Vanessa The New Yorker* magazine's Winthrop Sargeant said that Barber was "a real master of operatic tradition."

The premiere's cast included Eleanor Steber, the great American soprano, who is without a doubt one of the finest Mozart stylists of the past thirty years, and the fine mezzo Rosalind Elias.

Douglas Moore (1893–1969) is a genuinely creative musician who first attracted operatic attention with his *The Devil and Daniel Webster* in 1939. He was part of a fortunate time for American opera composers—the beginning of a period when they saw fit to face the necessity of breaking away from traditional, European opera *and* their own stubborn "America is the greatest" attitudes. They settled down to writing music that was a part of their distinctly individual selves.

Moore's *The Ballad of Baby Doe* was premiered in Central City, Colorado, in 1956, and had its first New York performance in 1958. The libretto by John Latouche is based on a true story of a famous beauty who was married to one of the country's richest men. She was discovered, in 1935, frozen to death near an abandoned silver mine. Moore has a genuine gift for melody, as many contemporary composers do not. The respected *New Yorker* commented about *Baby Doe:* "The result is a completely enchanting work of art—one that points to a bright future in which people will attend contemporary opera not out of a grim sense of cultural duty but simply because it is so infectious that they can't bear to stay away from it.

Gian-Carlo Menotti (1911–   ) recently stated in an interview for the English publication *Music and Musicians:* "I've done my fight. I'm tired. I've had enough. All the young critics are against me. They're poisonous. The operatic scene is too grueling." The gifted composer, librettist, stage director is now writing a play called *The Leper* which, he says, "reverses the fashionable theme of the duty of society to a minority and deals with the duty of the minority to society." Fortunately for American opera, Menotti wrote several successful works before he gave up—if indeed he has. His first opera was *Amelia Goes to the Ball* (1937). This was followed by *The Old Maid and the Thief* (1939) and *The Island God* (1942). In 1946 *The Medium* appeared and in 1947 *The Telephone.* Thus these two operas began their spectacular career that led to more than a thousand performances all over the world. Marie Powers was the medium, and her grand guignol interpretation is firmly set in the pages of music-theater history.

His powerful drama of life behind the Iron Curtain, *The Consul,* began its Broadway run in 1950. The superb singing actress Patricia Neway was Magda Sorel. Her intense performance and especially her magnificent singing of the big aria "To This We've Come," was greeted with a spontaneous ovation at *The Consul's* premiere—and at all the performances and revivals that have followed.

Brooks Atkinson, America's learned theater critic, called Menotti's next work, *The Saint of Bleecker Street* (1954), "a magnificent theatrical experience." Anina, the Saint, was sung by Virginia Gordoni.

The Medium, The Consul, and *The Saint of Bleecker Street* may pay homage to Puccini and Wagner, but they are works of theatrical genius and they show Menotti's special gifts for evoking—operatically—contemporary happenings in all their beauty and staggering sordidness.

Maria Golovin was presented in 1958, and his *The Last Savage,* had its Metropolitan premiere in 1964. Neither Menotti's stylish direction nor Beni Montresor's witty settings could disguise the fact that it was not a memorable work.

Menotti's last opera *Help! Help! The Globolinks!* was presented in Hamburg and in Sante Fe in 1969. Critics and public called it a masterpiece.

English opera appears to have reached its peak of contemporary creativity through the artistry of one composer in particular, but there are other British composers who are important. The incomparable comic genius of Sir Arthur Sullivan (1842–1900) and Sir William Gilbert (1836–1911) lives on in constantly popular performances of their many operettas such as *The Mikado, H.M.S. Pinafore, Iolanthe,* and *The Pirates of*

Penzance. Gilbert and Sullivan's impeccable and witty collaborations show evidence of being able to amuse audiences for another century.

Sir William Walton's (1902–   ) *Troilus and Cressida,* written when the composer was fifty-two, is an opera in the grand style, and it has been performed with success in London and San Francisco.

Arthur Benjamin's *A Tale of Two Cities* (1953), Sir Michael Tippet's *Midsummer Marriage* (1955), Richard Rodney Bennett's *The Mines of Sulphur* (1965), and Humphrey Searle's *Hamlet* (1968) are all significant operatic works, but none of them have quite achieved the level of the operas of Benjamin Britten.

Britten (1913–) is a pupil of Frank Bridge and John Ireland. All of his works, though they show honest admiration for Purcell and Stravinsky, are original. They also show his uncommon musical facility and ability to write for the voice. His knowledge of the orchestra and orchestration, in addition to his gifts as a conductor, make him unusual among modern composers. He began his professional career writing music for documentary films. His first major opera, *Peter Grimes* (1945), was made possible by a commission from famous conductor Serge Koussevitzky. At its American premiere in 1946, the conductor was Leonard Bernstein. *Peter Grimes* reached the Metropolitan in 1948 where its unimaginative setting and musical performance netted it a pallid reception it did not deserve. At its 1967 revival, the brilliant Colin Davis was at the helm, and the opera was a magnificent success. Jon Vickers sang the title role, but its creator, tenor Peter Pears, is considered the definitive interpreter of the part.

Britten's next opera, *The Rape of Lucretia,* was premiered (1946) at the jewel box of opera houses—Glyndebourne in Sussex. The part of the tragic Roman matron was sung by the indescribably beautiful contralto Kathleen Ferrier, who was also a striking *Orfeo.* Neville Cardus in *Kathleen Ferrier, a Memoir,* wrote: "Seldom has Covent Garden Opera House been so beautifully solemnized as when Kathleen Ferrier (Orpheus) flooded the place with tone which seemed as though classic shapes in marble were changing to melody, warm, rich-throated, but chaste." Britten called her interpretation of *Lucretia* "one of the most memorable of contemporary opera creations."

*Lucretia'*s American premiere took place at the now-demolished Ziegfeld Theater in 1948. Without a Ferrier in the leading role audiences have to work hard at appreciating the opera, and it has never been received as a truly popular work.

Albert Herring (1947) was first performed in the United States at the Berkshire Festival, Tanglewood. It is a comic chamber opera which critics seem to be at odds with—they claim it is either a comic masterpiece or a stumbling bore. *Billy Budd* (1951) is a work for male singers only. Its libretto is based on Herman Melville's novel about an inordinately handsome young seaman, Billy Budd, who is hanged for his accidental killing of a superior officer. At its premiere, the American baritone Theodore Uppman created the title role.

Gloriana (1953) was written for the coronation of Queen Elizabeth II of England. In it Britten and his librettist, William Plomer, have attempted to capture not only the character of Elizabeth I but the atmosphere of the Elizabethan epoch. Most critics agree that *Gloriana* is not top-drawer Britten, nor is *The Turn of the Screw* which was completed in 1954. *A Midsummer Night's Dream* (1960) takes its place next to *Peter Grimes* as a truly important opera. The libretto based on the familiar Shakespeare play was written by Britten and Peter Pears. It contains much effective music although one might quibble over the composer's use of so many treble voices. Since its Covent Garden performances in 1961, the opera has been heard in Holland, Germany, Yugoslavia, and the United States.

Britten's opera for young people—*The Little Sweep* (1949) and *Noye's Fludde* (1958)—show another facet of the composer's ingenuity and personality, as do his more recent Parables for Church Performance, *Curlew River, The Burning Fiery Furnace,* and *Prodigal Son.*

The versatile Britten continues to compose, and he continues to encourage young people in music. His *Young Person's Guide to the Orchestra* is a charming and informative introduction to all the instruments of the orchestra, and it should be noted that children's voices play a strong part in several of his works, namely, *Albert Herring, A Midsummer Night's Dream,* his children's operas, and *Curlew River.*

He also gives much of his time to performing, as a conductor, pianist, and accompanist, because he believes it is the only way to keep in contact with the all-important audience.

Britten is an idealist, both as a musician and a man. His idealism has not, however, cut him off from the times he lives in or the people he lives with. Following the first performances of his magnificent *War Requiem,* William Plomer wrote: "It was received as a work of vast scope, in which the composer, by giving it all the technical resources and emotional power at his command, so transcends the personal that he seems to comprehend the sufferings, to transfigure the grief, and to honor the potential goodness of humankind. It is addressed (and with what poignancy) to 'Whatever shares the eternal reciprocity of tears.' "

An illuminating statement by Clive Barnes of the *New York Times* seems to describe just a little bit more of what opera and its composers are all about. His critique of the Bolshoi ballerina Maya Plisetskaya includes: "I suppose Miss Plisetskaya is ballet's equivalent of the prima donna Maria Callas. To love them you must understand them a little—understand that they are not performing in any small minesculely perfect way, but rather offering all of themselves—miseries as well as grandeurs—to a unique projection of a role."

Great opera composers have made that offer too.

CHAPTER SEVENTEEN

The Producer, the Director, the Designers, and the Conductor

It is believed by some that the job of the opera producer-director is nothing more than moving the singing actors from place to place on the stage. They are far from correct.

Opera is probably the most complicated of all theater forms, and it requires experts all the way down the line—expert singers, conductors, orchestral musicians, scenic designers, costumers, and electricians. Therefore, pulling all these elements together and making them work is the incredibly difficult job of the producer. This statement does not ignore the fact that all these experts have been put at the disposal of the producer-director by an imaginative and strong-armed general manager. However, in this day of big business—and opera is a business as well as an art form—the manager prefers to concentrate his efforts on the organization. He keeps aloof from his artists and his staff and leaves the personal touch, the "bringing together," in the hands of the producer.

Because of this, the producer is not only held responsible for the stage movement—which includes building the drama and the action around the absolute necessity of the singers' always having contact with the conductor—he is responsible for scenic designs and costumes (either his own or those of the artists hired for a production) that enhance the opera and the singer. He must also be able to oversee the building of the sets and have a knowledge of selecting materials for and constructing the costumes. He should have a respectable musical knowledge and *know* when certain dramatic action will not work. And he should be able to discuss, with a hopefully cooperative conductor, the musical things that might not work for certain singers. In some cases producers are known to have a gift for making artists give more than is their normal best.

Dennis Arundell, the much admired English producer-director, has written: ". . . a producer has above all to be able to give all the collaborating experts their heads when desirable, and to check them gently but firmly—that is, tactfully—when necessary. It is rather like driving a team of fine, high mettled horses."

Joseph Urban (1872–1933) was one of the most remarkable designer-directors of operatic history. His revolutionary designs for Henry Russell's Boston Opera Company (1912–1913) are landmarks of the theater. He created more than fifty productions for the Metropolitan Opera, and he was a master of costuming and lighting. He was the first to do away with footlights and use lighting effects that enhanced the singers as well as the sets. He was a musician in addition to being a great designer, and he believed that "certain harmonic effects should be accentuated on the stage; the motif in the orchestra is my cue."

Jean Rosenthal was the lighting genius of contemporary theater. She lit more than two hundred Broadway shows and

many operas for the Metropolitan and the New York City Opera—as well as productions throughout the United States. She
said: "I have always believed that the use of light should be an
organic part of the stage effect, and the audience should not be
aware of the beauty of the light effect but of the beauty and
the appropriateness of the stage atmosphere. The leafy, mot-
tled forest light in the new Metropolitan *Hansel and Gretel*
was no happy accident; it was made possible because Nathaniel Merrill, the director, and Robert O'Hearn, the scenic designer, helped prepare the effect in advance.

"Light and music are a happy combination. Lighting for an
opera presents a great challenge, first because opera includes
all aspects of dance, drama, song and music; second because its
production organization is oriented toward a unified visual
whole solely concerned with providing proper atmosphere for
singer and music; third, because the production organization
is based on constantly changing repertory."

The Italian director Margherita Wallmann, who is the pride
of La Scala, is renowned for her spectacular productions.
When she staged the Met's new production of *La Gioconda,*
she said: "The opera is a wonderful museum piece. None of
the characters is really believable; they only live through the
music. This is a singers' opera. And singers get nervous in
great roles; it's hard to get them away from the conductor. I
was challenged by the enormous mass movements and the opportunity for show." One of her favorite works is Poulenc's
Les Dialogues des Carmélites. For, as she says: "For me, an
opera should have a spiritual message for the audience.

Another Italian, Franco Zeffirelli, is a gifted artist whose *Antony and Cleopatra* is better forgotten. However, his designs

and direction for *Falstaff, Cavalleria Rusticana,* and *Lucia di Lammermoor* are memorable opera contributions. He says: "I try to blow the dust away and re-create faithfully any work I produce, working from the music. One learns from each production, and takes a little bit of the previous production and incorporates it in the text. I am aiming at making the whole thing appear spontaneous. Of course it will be rehearsed down to the last detail, but the effect must be one of spontaneity, even of improvisation."

American Robert O'Hearn is the designing half of the Merrill-O'Hearn team that has given the new Met many magnificent productions that include *Die Meistersinger* and *The Woman Without a Shadow.* He is a meticulous and avid researcher who came to America's greatest opera house by way of the Broadway theater. He has come to realize that designing for opera is far more difficult than designing for plays or musical comedies. So many operas have been done for so many years that discovering a truly different approach is a tremendous challenge. His successes—and Nathaniel Merrill's as a stage director—prove that he has met the challenge.

German Rudolf Heinrich believes that opera and theater must be a part of the social architecture of one particular time. At thirty-eight he is one of the most controversial of designer-directors. His recent *Salome* kept the flames burning.

Another brilliant innovator is Tito Capobianco, whose *Tales of Hoffmann* production brought him to international attention. He has recently been appointed to head the Juilliard School Opera Theater.

A Callas performance—Kundry in *Parsifal*—turned film and stage director Luchino Visconti to opera. He recalls: "She was horribly costumed and wore a little pillbox hat that she kept batting back on her head as she sang. I said to myself right then, 'One day I'll work with you and you won't have to push hats out of your eyes.' A short time later I met her (1950) at Tullio Serafin's house. A big lady in a black suit." Visconti later directed Callas in several of her most spectacular European successes. Regarding his production of *The Marriage of Figaro* he says: "With Mozart you let yourself be guided by his music; when you deal with a genius you do not need to invent; you just put yourself at his service."

Visconti finds little difficulty in switching from films to opera. "After all each work of art is little more than a story of man, told to other men. The way you tell it, is the problem. Once you have that, most of your worries are over." He does not, however, want to see opera via the TV medium. "It's awful. Opera wasn't made to see a set of molars, dental fillings and a wiggling tongue. Close-ups destroy the mood, the feeling. Far from reviving an interest, it drives people to the movies, beaches or perhaps insane asylums."

Walter Felsenstein remains probably the most controversial of producer-directors. He has been the power behind the Komische Oper in Berlin for more than twenty years. Felsenstein was an actor before he became a producer in the theaters of Cologne, Munich and Zurich. His Berlin productions of *Carmen, Otello, The Tales of Hoffmann,* and *The Magic Flute* have been admired, acclaimed, and angrily denounced. Still there is no doubt that he is unique among operatic producers. He calls his productions "Realistic Theater of Music." In a published interview for *Music and Musicians* he stated: "Making the art of music and singing on the stage a convincing, sincere and indispensable human expression was and is the cardinal question, if one wants to speak of a theater of music at all. When a musical performance, staged by singers, becomes theatrical reality and unconditionally credible you have a theater of music. That means the dramatic event has to happen at an emotional level where music becomes the only means of expression."

He is a brilliant and dedicated artist and a far cry from the sensationalist he has been accused of being. His theater has done away with lazy tradition, and he refuses to accept anything unnatural "for the sake of the music." He is a ruthless taskmaster, but only because he is convinced that opera cannot exist on any stage without truth.

Herbert Graf is a more conventional producer. He was born in Vienna, and he is the son of the great music critic Max Graf. He staged operas in Philadelphia before joining the Metropolitan in 1936. He remained there for twenty-four years. He respects tradition, and most of his productions were and are in the "grand style." He is a thoroughly routined professional, has a way of handling crowd scenes, is patient with singers, and manages to imbue all his productions with a sense of nobility.

A producer who has no time for tradition is Tyrone Guthrie. He began directing for the Old Vic Theater Company in 1933 and joined the Sadler's Wells Opera (England) in 1941. He strives for naturalness in all his productions and has been known to show preference for honest acting from his singers rather than their being controlled by the musical demands of an opera. His productions of *Carmen* and *Traviata* for the Metropolitan in the 1950s caused much comment—both pro and con.

Sarah Caldwell is a veritable dynamo. Her imaginative productions in Boston have been acclaimed by press and public alike. In addition to being a producer-manager she often takes another step to establish her personal imprint on a production —she conducts. Her uncommon daring and picaresque person have made her the brunt of many dissenting comments. She did, however, bring American operagoers the premiere of *Moses und Aron* and a first rate *Falstaff,* just to mention two of her many productions. Her talent put her in the driver's seat of the American National Opera Company (1967–68). But as striking as her *Tosca* and *Lulu* productions were, she— like Mary Garden—proved that a theatrical imagination and musicality do not always make a general manager. The American National Opera Company lasted one ill-fated season on the road.

Greek actor Alexis Minotis also made opera news with his shattering production of *Medea* in Dallas in the 1950s.

And one of the great conductors, Herbert von Karajan, recently decided that he was a producer too. That leads us to the man, the master, the maestro who today is the king of the opera house—the conductor.

It is not possible in this volume to discuss all the conductors of opera who have enriched the form, but it is necessary to have a look at a few of the most important. Though it was not always so in the opera house, we know that today they reign supreme—in the rehearsal room and on the podium before their orchestra and singers.

Gustav Mahler (1860-1911) conducted in all the great opera houses of the world, including the Metropolitan, where he presented the first American performances of *The Queen of Spades* and *The Bartered Bride*. In addition to being the leading conductor of the Vienna Opera, he became the autocratic artistic director of that house in 1897. His ten years there proved that he was one of the truly great conductors and producers. He believed that clinging to outdated tradition was the next thing to slovenliness, and he demanded complete perfection from all his colleagues. He alone built the Vienna Opera ensemble into one of the musical monuments of the world. The revolutionary designer, Alfred Roller, was one of his artistic collaborators. The Mahler productions of *The Ring, Don Giovanni, Fidelio, The Magic Flute,* and *Falstaff* are considered by many to be the greatest interpretations these operas have been given.

Because Mahler was Jewish and because he was demanding —to the point of being considered a musical dictator—he had many enemies during his tenure in Vienna. But he still wiped out the Opera's incredible deficit and raised the standards of performance to a glorious height they had never known.

Arturo Toscanini (1876-1957) is a legend. He began his career as a cellist and became an overnight sensation when he replaced a conductor in Rio de Janeiro. The hostile audience stayed to cheer his performance of *Aïda* which he conducted from memory! Later, in Italy, he conducted the premieres of *Pagliacci* and *La Bohème* and introduced *The Ring* to that country. He became the leading conductor at La Scala in 1898 and held that position until 1902. He left that year because the audience booed him for not allowing encores.

For seven years, 1908–1915, he was the idol of the Metropolitan. Both Verdi and Puccini agreed that he understood their operas better than anyone. Because of his devotion to the composers' creations he became—to some—an unbearable tyrant. The story goes that the glamorous soprano Geraldine Farrar instructed the Maestro to follow her in a certain musical passage. She informed him that *she* was the star. "Madame," he replied, "the only stars I know are those in heaven!"

His Salzburg performances of *Falstaff* and *Fidelio* (with Lotte Lehmann as Leonora), following his departure from La Scala because of his open disagreement with Mussolini, are a part of history.

In New York, 1944–54, he conducted unforgettable concert performances of several operas, including his favorites, *Otello, La Bohème,* and *La Traviata.* His domineering musical personality and volatile temper often directed him into torrential rages. But all who worked with him and heard his music agree that he was a genius who enriched the opera world.

Tullio Serafin (1878–1968) was a great gentleman of music. He began his career in 1900 and continued to conduct until just a few years before his death. He was on the podium for the first Italian *Wozzeck* and the Scala premiere of *Der Rosenkavalier.* He could not be equaled as a conductor of Bellini, Rossini, and Verdi. Young singers and musicians adored him, and he encouraged them to approach the great operas with the same humility as he did. He would not allow carelessness in rehearsals or performances. But his kindly soul always saw to it that any singer who, by accident or unexpected stage business, went astray was brought back into the musical fold.

Serafin conducted the premieres of Deems Taylor's *The*

King's Henchman and *Peter Ibbetson* at the Metropolitan. He also conducted the American premiere of *Turandot* at that theater.

He was extremely helpful to Rosa Ponselle, and he was the guiding force behind Callas. It was he who encouraged her to become a dramatic coloratura. Later he coached Joan Sutherland for her Covent Garden *Lucia*.

He was a great musician and a great human being.

The amazing Austrian, Herbert von Karajan (1908–) is a remarkable conductor and a matinee-idol personality. He speeds through Europe in his red Jaguar, flies his own plane, and lately produces many of the operas he conducts.

He made his debut in 1928 with *The Marriage of Figaro* and by 1948 he was an important figure at La Scala. Vienna made him the artistic director of the State Opera in 1956. He added the same position at the Salzburg Festival to his crown of achievements in 1958. He conducts the Strauss-Wagner-Mozart repertory as well as operas like *Lucia* and *Trovatore*. He resembles all ambitious artists and is often inclined to get carried away. His *Boris* may be triumphant, but his *Carmen* is far from ideal.

The Metropolitan witnessed his conducting and saw his production of *Die Walküre* and *Das Rheingold* during the 1967–68 and 1968–69 seasons, and as usual the critics disagreed as to whether they were dark, grim neo-Bayreuth productions or ones illuminated by genius. Musically, they were typically von Karajan—different and personal. Above all they were lyric and youthfully passionate—the work of a masterful conductor-producer.

Leonard Bernstein was born in 1918. He is the New York

reincarnation of the Renaissance man—dynamic conductor, colorful composer, articulate writer, and the idol of millions of symphony and opera fans. He was the conductor for the Visconti-Callas productions of *Medea* and *La Sonnambula* at La Scala in 1954 and 1955.

Bernstein was on the podium for the Zeffirelli *Falstaff* at the Metropolitan and received forty curtain calls for his conducting of *Der Rosenkavalier* in Vienna in 1968. There were those who suspected that he might have finally met his fate by attempting to lead that aristocratic and dogmatic orchestra through performances of a work so close to their traditional Viennese hearts. But he came out of them more wildly acclaimed than ever. There is no reason to believe however, that simply because the Viennese now regard him as their "Lenny" that his American fans will ever release him.

Thanks are extended to all the conductors—from the beginning of opera to the ones who are just beginning—young or old, they *are,* as they say in the opera houses of the world, the Maestros.

Acting in Opera

BY REGINA RESNIK

More than ever before, the thespian aspects of opera are assuming greater proportions and importance. But there is so much more that can be done if we are truly to make the operatic stage a living, vibrant force in the entertainment world of today.

Foremost is the fact that the actor on the legitimate stage is there because he has a "calling"—he *wants* to be an actor. The singer acting on the operatic stage is there because he has a gift to sing and wants to sing, but not necessarily to act. Indeed, he may have little liking or no special talent for acting. Too, the nature and repertoire of opera demand that the opera singer, who is "typecast," so to speak, mostly by voice alone, master a far greater variety of characterizations than the legitimate actor. Few singers in opera play only "themselves." A young coloratura may perhaps be cast over and over as Gilda, Lucia, Rosina, etc. But the majority of opera singers must be prepared as performers to run the gamut of age and personality. Within the past several years, at the Metropolitan and in other opera houses in Europe, I have portrayed gypsies, young and old, such as Carmen, Ulrica, Azucena, and Czipra. I was the ludicrous spinster in *Figaro,* the tragic Klytemnästra, the old grandmother in *Vanessa,* the young princess Amneris, Prince Orlofsky, and Herodias. Moreover during my "first" career as a soprano I had the good fortune also to portray Aïda, the *Trovatore* Leonora, Chrysothemis, both Frasquita and Micaëla, the *Valkyrie* Helmwige, and Sieglinde (now Fricka) and Rosalinda as well.

Another problem of acting on the operatic stage rises from the fact that, despite the wide range of portrayals in the repertoire, many of the roles are static; they are not "living flesh." They may go through various emotional tribulations, but there is no particular character development. They are the same persons at the end of the opera (whether dead or alive!) as they were at the beginning. Add, too, the fact that the opera singer is limited in his acting by the composer's wishes. His conception of a role must conform to the phrasing of the music and the words that are sung. An Othello on the legitimate stage takes his life and does it in a few phrases which take possibly a minute or less of spoken dialogue. The opera singer, however, must linger over such action through several pages of music. These are some, though not all, of the problems of acting on the operatic stage. A poorly or stiffly acted opera, however magnificently sung, will not satisfy the modern audience. There is no denying the need for voices in opera, but a vibrantly dramatic performance will add immeasurably to it.

Certainly, opera singers are paying more attention to the basic rudiments of acting and appearance in order to give better performances. But the opera singer ought to realize that he is, in reality, a singing actor, and think of himself as such constantly. It is not enough any longer to simply learn the barest rudiments of acting—though that alone, in some cases, would create a vast improvement. Today's singing actor needs more than the old instruction pertaining to body movement, how to talk, stand still, bow, kneel, fall, draw a sword, kiss the soprano. This may have sufficed when little besides singing was expected of the opera singer; but no longer.

Writing in *The Technique of Operatic Acting,* Bennett Challis states: "Intensity and continuity of dramatic line are of utmost importance in musical drama (as in all true drama) and should be the singing-actor's most cherished ideals." In considering the importance of acting on the operatic stage, it is of course understood that movements and gestures are directed by the music, and that the music, adding artistically and emotionally to what the words express, offers additional motivational clues. The composer's music and the libretto are set factors, but the singing actor is not imprisoned within them anymore than the legitimate actor is imprisoned by the playwright's lines. With full understanding of the character he is portraying and of the scene, be it one of pathos or comedy, he can, within the limits of the established music and words, enhance the performance. Despite the problems so unique to the operatic stage, operatic acting need not be mere pantomime (frequently traditionally "hammy" pantomime!) set to music, and the opera singer need not be a puppet. The history of opera reveals that only a choice few have gained fame by relying solely on voice. Today's young opera singer is being increasingly measured by his talent as an actor as well as a singer.

The influence of the Broadway musical, motion pictures, and television has "taught" the opera fan today to expect more than just a voice.

The problems of acting on the operatic stage can be mastered with diligent and intelligent application. The ambitious young opera singer can and must learn more than just the basic fundamentals of acting. He must learn not merely how to handle himself physically but also how to interpret a role, how to integrate himself into the entire performance, how to project most genuinely and naturally—for himself and thus for the audience. A beautiful voice, combined with the proper physical attributes for a particular role, is certainly to be desired! And today's opera singers are more conscious of their appearance than ever before. Even so, there are "tricks of the trade"—as, for example, a high hairdo or wig, built-up shoes, and so forth. Still, once the singer is established, such possible physical adjuncts on the operatic stage will tend to be overlooked more than on the legitimate stage. Opera is no longer just music. It cannot afford to be. It is drama, with the music and the instrument of the voice adding a thrilling dimension and emotion to what the spoken word alone cannot express. Not everyone can be a Caruso to whom the art of acting was inborn and instinctive, nor a Pinza who was able to project his own personality into any role he was playing and make it a brilliant characterization.

There are many excellent teachers who can teach acting to singers. But as yet there is no established school devoted to the subject. The growth of the "opera workshops" is an important step in the right direction. Mary Garden, one of the greatest operatic actresses, is reputed to have said: "Take care of the dramatic line and the musical line will take care of itself." I quite agree with this. The voice may be the paramount thing, but stagecraft and dramatic interpretation make opera a thrilling and complete experience.

Mezzo-soprano Regina Resnik was born in New York City of Ukrainian parents. The role of her Metropolitan Opera debut was Leonora in *Il Trovatore*. The occasion was a theatrical one; with only twenty-four hours notice Resnik substituted for Zinka Milanov! As her career progressed she sang most of the major roles in the soprano repertory. But, as she says: "In 1954 I came to find myself more comfortable in the darker, more dramatic qualities of the soprano voice . . . the center or pivot of my voice became A and B, the true mezzo center." She has been heard and acclaimed in the major opera houses of the world. Her continuing recognition as a truly important singing-actress makes her comments on operatic acting particularly valid.

Important Conductors

Otto Ackermann
Franz Allers
Sir John Barbirolli
Sir Thomas Beecham
Vincenzo Bellezza
Karl Böhm
Artur Bodanzky
Richard Bonynge
Pierre Boulez
Fritz Busch
André Cluytens
Fausto Cleva
Colin Davis
Victor de Sabata
Issay Dobrowen
Ferenc Fricsay
Wilhelm Furtwängler
Vittorio Gui
Rudolf Kempe
Erich Kleiber
Otto Klemperer
Hans Knappertsbusch
Clemens Krauss
Josef Krips

Erich Leinsdorf
Lorin Maazel
Zubin Mehta
Francesco Molinari-Pradelli
Ettore Panizza
Jonel Perlea
Giorgio Polacco
Georges Prêtre
Fritz Reiner
Artur Rodzinski
Hans Rosbaud
Wolfgang Sawallisch
Hermann Scherchen
Thomas Scherman
Thomas Schippers
Alexander Smallens
Georg Solti
Fritz Stiedry
Leopold Stokowski
George Szell
Heinz Tietjen
Arturo Toscanini
Bruno Walter
Felix Weingartner

The Voices

The types of voices you will hear in opera are:

THE SOPRANO

The highest of female voices with a range that generally encompasses two octaves—from middle C to high C. Modern audiences are accustomed to *different* types of sopranos:

a. the dramatic—a darker, heavier type of voice usually capable of singing roles like Elektra, Isolde, and Turandot.

b. the lyric—a clear, sweet voice which is lighter in texture and sound than the dramatic. Micaëla, Mimi, Pamina, and Violetta are roles suited to this voice.

c. the spinto—a heavy lyric voice. Tosca, Butterfly, Aïda, Manon Lescaut are roles that sound best in the spinto voice.

d. the coloratura—a light, agile soprano voice capable of great feats of vocal dexterity. The range of the coloratura is usually extended several notes above high C.

THE MEZZO-SOPRANO

From the Italian word *mèzzo* (half). A female voice halfway between the soprano and the contralto.

THE CONTRALTO

A lower, darker, and heavier female voice. The range is generally from G below middle C to two octaves above—with a possible A or B-flat extension.

THE TENOR

The highest male voice. From the Latin word *tenere* (to hold). In early polyphonic music this voice held the melody while other voices worked in counterpoint. There are types of tenor voices: the dramatic, the lyric, the spinto, and the heldentenor (heroic tenor much desired for Wagnerian roles).

THE BARITONE

The male voice between the tenor and the bass. Also categorized as lyric or dramatic. Some heldentenors are graduates from the high baritone field—namely, the great Lauritz Melchior and Ramon Vinay.

THE BASS

The lowest of male voices. His music (and the baritone's) is written in the bass clef which indicates F below middle C as the top line. A particular type of bass voice is the basso cantante—lyric or singing bass, such as Ezio Pinza and Cesare Siepi.

The Terms

You will hear these voices singing:

ARIA

From the Italian word for *air, song*. Of the several types the most important are—

The aria cantabile—a song whose movement is generally slow. It expresses tenderness and pathos.

The aria parlante—more declamatory in style and better suited to expressing violent emotions and passion.

The aria di bravura—in allegro tempo, with brilliant sections of coloratura and vocal embellishments.

The aria da capo—used particularly by Handel. The first section is always repeated following a section of contrast.

CABELETTA

A short operatic song with a brisk pace. Verdi used the cabaletta as a quick, final section of an aria; e.g., the cabalettas ending *"Tacea la notte"* (*Il Trovatore*) and *"Ernani, Involami"* (*Ernani*).

DUET

A combination of two voices; e.g., the flower duet from *Madame Butterfly* (Puccini).

TRIO

A combination of three voices; e.g., the closing trio in *Der Rosenkavalier* (Strauss).

QUARTET

A combination of four voices; e.g., the final scene of *Rigoletto* (Verdi).

COMPRIMARIO ROLE

A secondary operatic role often requiring a singer of great versatility and dramatic ability.

CRESCENDO

By control of the breath the singer is able to increase the loudness of the tone. The exact opposite is decrescendo (from the Italian *to lessen*).

ENCORE

Term meaning perform it again. The French use *bis*—from the word *bisser*—meaning to repeat. No matter what language, the practice is not tolerated at the Metropolitan Opera House.

ENSEMBLES

A musical number for several voices. From the French meaning together. More importantly used to describe the teamwork of an opera company. Such as: The ensemble of the house is poor.

FALSETTO

A method used primarily by tenors to create tones in a register that is higher than their normal range.

FERMATA

A term meaning pause or hold. It is marked thus over a note ⌒, often called a "birdseye" in popular music. Sometimes indulged in (in Italian opera) to the point of absurdity—not so much today when the conductor is king.

FLAT

A term meaning below proper pitch. With singers it can be the result of poor training, a bad ear, or vocal fatigue. Its opposite is sharp, a term meaning above the proper pitch.

FORTE, FORTISSIMO

From the Italian meaning loud, very loud.

HEAD VOICE

A register of the voice in which the singer feels the tone vibrating in the head. A direct contrast to the chest voice.

INTERVAL

Meaning the distance between a low note and a higher one; e.g., the interval from C up to G is called a fifth.

LEGATO

From the Italian meaning bound together. The notes of a phrase or line in an aria are sung with great smoothness. Its opposite is staccato.

MESSA DI VOCE

Italian term for placing the voice. A steady crescendoing and diminuendoing of volume on one note. When effectively done it is most beautiful, and it also shows the extent of the singer's technique.

PIANO, PIANISSIMO

Italian for soft, very soft.

TRILL

An ornamentation usually marked with *tr* ⌇⌇⌇ over the note. It consists of rapid alternations between a note and the one above it. Singers with a good trill are very rare today.

VIBRATO

From the Italian meaning vibrated. It is a rapid, fluctuating sound that, with singers, is sometimes recognized as a "wobble." Not to be confused with a tremolo which is a heightening of intensity in the singing tone.

Renowned Singers

Christine Nilsson
Sofia Scalchi
Marcella Sembrich
Marianne Brandt
Anton Schott
Hermann Weber
Lilli Lehmann
Max Alvary
Emil Fischer
Albert Niemann
Minnie Hauk
Édouard de Reszke
Jean de Reszke
Emma Eames
Lillian Nordica
Emma Calvé
Victor Maurel
Francesco Tamagno
Zélie de Lussan
Sibyl Sanderson
Nellie Melba

David Bispham
Andreas Dippel
Johanna Gadski
Anton Van Rooy
Ernestine Schumann-Heink
Louise Homer
Fritzi Scheff
Milka Ternina
Lucienne Bréval
Olive Fremstad
Pol Plançon
Marcel Journet
Enrico Caruso
Celestina Boninsegna
Lina Cavalieri
Geraldine Farrar
Feodor Chaliapin
Riccardo Martin
Giannina Arangi-Lombardi
Anna Bahr-Mildenburg
Gemma Bellincioni

Alessandro Bonci

Hariclea Darclée

Fernando de Lucia

Célestine Galli-Marié

Margaretre Siems

Pasquale Amato

Frances Alda

Emmy Destinn

Mariette Mazarin

Antonio Scotti

Edmond Clément

Leo Slezak

Alma Gluck

Elvira de Hidalgo

Léon Rothier

Luisa Tetrazzini

Jacques Urlus

Lucrezia Bori

Frieda Hempel

Marguerite Namara

Giovanni Martinelli

Elisabeth Schumann

Edith Mason

Paul Althouse

Giuseppe de Luca

Florence Austral

Maria Barrientos

Toti Dal Monte

Claire Dux

Mary Garden

Maria Ivogün

Adele Kern

Conchita Supervia

Claudia Muzio

John McCormack

Margaret Matzenauer

Florence Easton

Rosa Ponselle

Beniamino Gigli

Anne Roselle

Giuseppe Danise

Amelita Galli-Curci

Armand Tokatyan

Maria Jeritza

Queena Mario

Sigrid Onegin

Elisabeth Rethberg

Marion Telva

Edward Johnson

Lawrence Tibbett

Karin Branzell

Max Altglass

Giacomo Lauri-Volpi

Maria Müller

Lauritz Melchior

Titta Ruffo

Rosa Raïsa

George Cehanovsky

Ezio Pinza

Richard Mayr

Maggie Teyte

Friedrich Schorr

Germaine Lubin

Gertrude Kappel

Dorothee Manski

Grete Stückgold

Leonora Corona

Gladys Swarthout

Grace Moore
Georges Thill
Lily Pons
Mafalda Favero
Anny Konetzni
Hilde Konetzni
Helge Roswänge
Tiana Lemnitz
Ninon Vallin
Frederick Jagel
Max Lorenz
Göta Ljungberg
Tito Schipa
Frida Leider
Maria Olszewska
Richard Bonelli
Lotte Lehmann
Coe Glade
Kirsten Flagstad
Helen Jepson
Rose Bampton
Richard Crooks
Julius Huehn
Emanuel List
John Charles Thomas
Marjorie Lawrence
Thelma Votipka
Gertrude Wettergren
Lina Pagliughi
Marta Fuchs
René Maison
Irene Jessner
Irra Petina
Bidu Sayão

Helen Traubel
John Brownlee
Jan Kiepura
Gina Cigna
Dusolina Giannini
Kerstin Thorborg
Herbert Janssen
Charles Kullmann
Leonard Warren
Maria Caniglia
Zinka Milanov
Rosa Pauly
Risë Stevens
Carolina Segrera
Bruna Castagna
Georges Cathelat
Alexander Kipnis
Licia Albanese
Winifred Heidt
Jarmila Novotna
Stella Roman
James Melton
Raoul Jobin
Ina Souez
Salvatore Baccaloni
Erna Berger
Hans Hotter
Elisabeth Grümmer
Margarete Klose
Jussi Bjoerling
Robert Weede
Alexander Sved
Eleanor Steber
Maria Cebotari

Kurt Baum
Lily Djanel
Astrid Varnay
Jan Peerce
Margaret Harshaw
Richard Tauber
Ebe Stignani
Martial Singher
Patrice Munsel
Richard Tucker
Regina Resnik
Blanche Thebom
Torsten Ralf
Set Svanholm
Dorothy Kirsten
Daniza Ilitsch
Robert Merrill
Roberta Peters
Tito Gobbi
Hilde Gueden
Martha Mödl
Magda Olivero
Clara Petrella
Maria Reining
Viorica Ursuleac
Claramae Turner
Joan Hammond
Elisabeth Höngen
Ljuba Welitsch
Elisabeth Schwarzkopf
Constance Shacklock
Giulietta Simionato
Ferruccio Tagliavini
Christl Goltz

Nicola Rossi-Lemeni
Marianna Radev
Irene Dalis
Renata Scotto
Amy Shuard
Cesare Siepi
Antonietta Stella
Joan Sutherland
Hermann Uhde
Ramon Vinay
Theodor Uppman
Nell Rankin
Kathleen Ferrier
Gerda Lammers
Richard Lewis
Peter Pears
Renata Tebaldi
Lucine Amara
Jon Vickers
Peter Anders
Fedora Barbieri
Marian Anderson
David Ward
Raphael Arié
Rita Gorr
Ernst Häfliger
Inge Borkh
Carlos Alexander
Marie Powers
Gré Brouwenstijn
Boris Christoff
Maria Callas
Elisabeth Carron
Eileen Farrell

Franco Corelli
Régine Crespin
Lisa Della Casa
Mario Del Monaco
Giuseppe di Stefano
Teresa Berganza
Victoria de los Angeles
Denise Duval
Mattiwilda Dobbs
Nicolai Gedda
Galina Vishnevskaya
Geraint Evans
Dietrich Fischer-Dieskau
Gérard Souzay
Sándor Kónya
Helga Pilarczyk
Leonie Rysanek
Leontyne Price
Jean Madeira
Christa Ludwig
Walter Berry
Gabriella Tucci

Teresa Stich-Randall
Rita Streich
Fritz Wunderlich
Marie Collier
Guus Hoekmann
George London
Wolfgang Windgassen
Birgit Nilsson
Nicolai Ghiaurov
Jess Thomas
Thomas Stewart
Evelyn Lear
James McCracken
Helen Watts
Josephine Veasey
Marilyn Horne
Elena Suliotis
James King
Monserrat Caballé
Ingrid Bjoner
Grace Bumbry
Martina Arroyo

Bibliography

The World of Opera, Brockway and Weinstock; Pantheon, 1962

The Metropolitan Opera, Irving Kolodin; Knopf, 1966

A Short History of Opera, Donald Jay Grout; Columbia, 1966

The Flagstad Manuscript, Louis Biancolli; Putnam, 1952

Maria Callas, Eugenio Gara; Kister, 1958

Callas: La Divina, Stelios Galatopoulos; J. M. Dent, 1966

Opera Annual No. 8; Lyle Stuart, 1962

A Working Friendship; Random House, 1961

Glyndebourne, Spike Hughes; Methuen, 1966

A History of the Opera in the Middle West, R. L. Davis, Prentice-Hall, 1965

How Opera Grew, Peyser and Bauer; Putnam, 1956

Journey Towards Music, Victor Gollancz; Dutton, 1965

Listen Here, Vernon Duke; Obolensky, 1963

The Price of Genius, April Fitzlyon; Appleton-Century, 1964

Richard Strauss, William Mann; Cassell & Co., 1964

Opera, Harold Rosenthal, Editor; Rolls House (monthly)

Opera News, Frank Merkling, Editor; Opera News (monthly)

Ring Resounding, John Culshaw; Viking, 1967

Austria: Land of Music; Federal Press Service of Vienna

Men of Music, Brockway and Weinstock; Simon and Schuster, 1962

The Great Singers, Henry Pleasants; Simon and Schuster, 1966

Mozart, Alfred Einstein; Oxford, 1944

Debussy, Oscar Thompson; Dodd, Mead, 1937

Mary Garden's Story, Louis Biancolli; Simon and Schuster, 1951

Wagner as Man and Artist, Ernest Newman; Garden City, 1941

The Letters of Richard Wagner; Knopf, 1932

Grove's Dictionary of Music and Musicians; Macmillan, 1880 and 1949

Opera Dictionary, Rosenthal and Warrack; Oxford University, 1964

Metropolitan Opera Annals, William H. Seltsam; H. W. Wilson, 1947

Gustav Mahler, Alma Mahler; Viking, 1946

Mozart, the Man and his Works, W. J. Turner; Knopf, 1945

Pantomime, Wallace Fowlie; Regnery, 1951

Janáček, Hans Hollander; Calder Books, 1963

"Orff's *Antigonae*"—An Introduction by Wolfgang Schadewaldt; Little Orchestra Society, Program Notes, 1968

Baker's Biographical Dictionary of Musicians, Nicholas Slonimsky; G. Schirmer, 1965

Opera 66; Alan Ross, 1966

International Encyclopedia of Music and Musicians, Oscar Thompson; Dodd, Mead, 1946

Kobbé's Complete Opera Book, Edited by the Earl of Harwood; Putnam, 1963

A Handbook of American Operatic Premieres 1713–1962, Julius Mattfeld; Detroit Studies in Music Bibliography, 1963

Fifty Years of Opera and Ballet in Italy; Carlo Bestetti, 1963

The Stage Works of Richard Strauss; Boosey & Hawkes, 1944

My Lord, What a Morning, Marian Anderson; Viking, 1956

Opera, Edward J. Dent; Penguin, 1949

The Life of Richard Wagner (four volumes), Ernest Newman; Knopf, 1933–46

Verdi: His Life and Works, Francis Toye; Knopf, 1931

The Great Conductors, Harold C. Shonberg; Simon and Schuster, 1967

"Richard Wagner: The Man and His Music" *High Fidelity,* November, 1966

"Munich and Its Sometimes Favorite Son," Paul Moor; *High Fidelity,* June, 1964

"The Paradox of 'Late Strauss,'" George R. Marek and Patrick J. Smith; *High Fidelity,* June, 1964

Index